EXCEL WITH PYTHON: UNLOCK YOUR INNER RANGE

Hayden Van Der Post

Reacative Publishing

To my daughter, may she know anything is possible.

CONTENTS

Title Page

Dedication

Chapter 1: Introduction to Python and Excel   1

Chapter 2: Setting-up Your Development Environment   12

Chapter 3: Python Basics   22

Chapter 4: Excel Essentials   33

Chapter 5: Interacting Between Python and Excel   45

Chapter 6: In-depth Python for Excel   60

Chapter 8: Advanced Data Analysis   86

Chapter 10: Automating Excel Tasks with Python   113

Chapter 11: Real-world Projects   130

Chapter 12: Conclusion and Going Beyond   146

CHAPTER 1: INTRODUCTION TO PYTHON AND EXCEL

There exist distinct tools with diverse capabilities in the computer universe, but few duos can match the remarkable prowess that Python and Excel ally to form. This liaison of two technological giants is a bounty to those who wish to leapfrog their productivity competence, elevating efficiency, and expanding the boundaries of what's plausible with everyday tasks.

Python, originating from the multifaceted world of programming, brings an entourage of capabilities to the computational arena. At the heart of Python's uniqueness lies its elegant simplicity and versatility. Inherently approachable, this high-level, general-purpose programming language becomes an empowering tool for novices and a wellspring of creativity for veterans. From data analysis to web development, to artificial Intelligence, Python adapts flamboyantly to a glut of applications.

When coupled with Excel, an application hailed for its robustness in handling data analytics and graphical features, Python's prowess expands exponentially. Excel shines bright in the business world where it is synonymous with managing data, performing complex calculations, and creating professional reports. As an electronic spreadsheet, it can contain vast amounts of numerical data, manipulate them through formulas, and visually represent the data via graphs and charts.

Yet, Excel is more than just a spreadsheet. In its essence, Excel is a microcosm that enables professionals--from business analysists to finance experts--to unravel useful insights from figures and statistics with little programming knowledge. With features like PivotTables and Power BI, Excel transforms columns of numbers into interpretable data, affirming itself as the go-to tool for business intelligence.

Meanwhile, Python serves as the heart, pumping life into Excel's static data. Able to interact with Excel's environment seamlessly, Python extends Excel's functionality further than conventionally feasible. With the simplicity of Python syntax and the power of its libraries, it quickly sifts through dunes of data, making it an indispensable tool in any data scientist's arsenal. Python becomes the chef d'oeuvre, taking cooking (data) to the heart, slicing (analyzing), sorting, and sautéing (visualizing) to serve a Michelin star dinner (intuitive insights).

When Python's dynamism melds with Excel's formidable analytical prowess, it forms an impressive synergy, like a well-rehearsed symphony orchestra playing a melodious symphony. You will witness how the precision of Python can mine valuable insights in the blink of an eye. Imagine feeding Python with tons of Excel data, and letting it play with this feast, using in-built functions to identify trends, deduce patterns, or predict future behaviors. It's essentially placing the might of Python's automation and computing rigor in the hands of Excel users.

Caution though! Like learning to conduct the orchestra, your journey through these chapters requires patience. Mastery doesn't happen overnight. As you progress through the chapters, you'll adopt the rhythm and pace at which Python and Excel dance together, and you'll soon realize how these seemingly contrasting tools harmonize like a carefully composed melody.

The world of Python and Excel beckons you; an avenue of opportunities ripe with potential for your professional enhancement. As you read further, you'll uncover how Python and Excel join forces to make your work more efficient, accurate, and impactful. With each page turned, you'll step closer to mastering this dance, the Python & Excel Tango.

Possible Applications

As the adage goes, necessity is indeed the mother of invention. The sprawling digital plain has ushered forth a rigid demand for advanced data handling and computational utility. To remain relevant, one must master the nuances of data analysis, simulation, algorithmic efficiency, even machine learning; all within the framework of our trusted assistant, Excel, supplemented deftly with the might of Python.

To begin, consider the heritage of modern business intelligence - data analysis. With Excel's built-in functionality, industries can toss a diverse range of numerical data into the program and gain basic but essential insights through its charts and formulas. Now, imagine drizzling this straightforward process with the versatility of Python. Suddenly, large datasets are not intimidating. Python's ability to swiftly analyze big data transmutes 'data-fatigue' into a pursuit of meaningful understanding, transforming apparently confusing figures into clear, effective business strategies.

When scripting with Python, Excel mellows to a softer beat, the barriers surrounding complex calculations melt away. You will watch in awe as sophisticated financial models halt their beleaguering nature, easing into Python smoothed equations. Suddenly, risk models, solvency equations, or propensity algorithms dance to your tunes like obedient soldiers, marching in sync with the beat of your Python-powered baton.

Ever envisaged using Python for simulation? The world of Excel opens up to a galaxy of potential when Python steps in. Through Python's intricate libraries, Monte Carlo Simulations, or even complex linear programming methods become attainable, and Econometric models, formerly intricate and sphinx-like, strive to make sense readily.

As industries propel towards automation, Python extends its warm hand, promising to carry Excel users into this promising future. Whether it's automating boring data entry tasks, extracting data from other sources, or churning out routinely needed reports at chosen intervals, Python grants Excel the gift of automation. A gift that saves time, increases productivity, and most importantly, lets you focus on tasks that really matter.

But what about machine learning? With the advent of AI, industries and businesses are increasingly leaning on predictive analysis. Python, with its powerful libraries like scikit-learn or TensorFlow, can inject your Excel with machine learning capabilities. With this augmented power, you could predict customer behavior, forecast sales, or even detect fraudulent activities.

In the realm of web scraping, Excel and Python form the perfect alliance. Python, with its keen libraries like Beautiful Soup or Scrappy, can skim data from the web, and with Excel waiting to analyze this large influx, business intelligence moves towards a new horizon.

From academia to finance, healthcare to retail, or the buzzing start-ups in Silicon Valley, every industry will benefit from the combined strengths of Python and Excel. It helps elevate productivity, revolutionize efficiency and change the way we handle, analyze, and visualize data.

As your proficiency grows, you'll discover the applications of Python and Excel are only limited by the scope of your imagination. The potential is astronomical, the capabilities infinite and the revolution, inevitable. As we journey together through this book, we'll unlock these applications, one chapter at a time.

The Importance Of Combining Them

In today's rapidly evolving technological landscape, the harmonization of Python and Excel brings unprecedented value. Given how ubiquitous these platforms have become, their alliance facilitates the amalgamation of flexibility and functionality - a powerful cocktail that's tailored to suit any professional environment. As we're delving into the significance of uniting these tools, picture yourself cultivating a garden. Excel is the soil, fertile and ready. Python, on the other hand, is the skilled gardener, ready to nurture and transform the soil into a bountiful landscape.

Excel, despite its capabilities, has its limitations. While it's well-equipped to handle small to moderately large data sets and perform basic data analysis, things can turn cumbersome with massive datasets. Computationally intensive tasks may make your spreadsheets sluggish. The software is, intrinsically, not designed for speed. This is where Python comes into play. With its high-performing algorithms and ability to handle vast, tangled datasets, the Pythonic touch ensures that Excel overcomes its performance hurdle.

Beyond performance, Python heightens Excel's capabilities by several notches. As a general-purpose language, Python is blessed with a variety of libraries. Such libraries cater to a multitude of needs - from data analysis (pandas, NumPy) and visualization (matplotlib, seaborn) to machine learning (scikit-learn, TensorFlow) and web scraping (Beautiful Soup, Scrapy). By integrating these libraries with Excel, you have a potent blend that's capable of tackling the most intricate data tasks.

Automation is another aspect where Python augments Excel's abilities. Say goodbye to those long, weary hours spent updating data, creating reports, or other repetitive tasks in Excel. With Python, you can script this tedium into oblivion, freeing you up to concentrate on more complex, value-adding jobs.

Let's also talk about cost-effectiveness and accessibility. Python, being an open-source language, ensures that businesses and individuals alike can reap its benefits without worrying about licensing costs. Combine that with the widespread familiarity with Excel across workspaces, and you have a toolkit that's beneficial without introducing new software or insurmountable learning curves.

Successfully interweaving Python and Excel allows us to transcend the traditional, manual paradigm of data handling. We propel ourselves into an era where data analysis becomes agile, modelling turns more reliable, and decision-making processes more informed and efficient. Such an evolution amplifies the professional capacities of individuals across varied sectors. Be it the financial analyst deriving complex risk models, the academic researcher simulating statistical phenomena, the data scientist wrangling with big data, or the retail manager predicting future sales trends - combining Python and Excel is the ace up their sleeves.

Recognizing the inherent value that Python and Excel bring to the realm of data manipulation and analysis is merely the first step. What's imperative is the subsequent pursuit of proficiency in their combined application. As we further delve into this book, we'll equip you with the knowledge and skills to fluently speak the language of Python and Excel. With every chapter of this manual, we aim to set your fears aside and replace them with the empowerment that this powerful duo brings to the world. Let's continue this enlightening voyage into the next section, where we will explore popular instances of automation using Python and Excel.

Popular Automation Examples

As we journey further into the amalgamation of Python and Excel, let's shine a spotlight on some popular examples of automation. These instances demonstrate the synergy between these tools and how they serve to maximize efficiency, reduce redundancy, and enhance analytical capabilities within different professional contexts.

1. **Data Cleaning and Transformation**: The first step in any data analysis project is to ensure that the data at hand is clean and correctly formatted. Think of it as sorting and organizing ingredients before cooking a meal. Python, with its libraries like pandas and NumPy, is a formidable force in data cleaning. From identifying and handling missing values, transforming data types, handling outliers or synthesis of new features, Python arms Excel with an extensive toolkit to deal with any messy data

scenario you come across.

2. **Report Generation**: Remember those long hours spent in creating weekly, monthly, or quarterly reports manually in Excel? Let's say adieu to that old grind! With Python, you can automate report generation, including charts and pivot tables. Once you've written the script, it's as simple as clicking a button. Add to that, Python's ability to churn out customizable, dynamic and visually appealing reports (thanks to the matplotlib and seaborn libraries), and you have yourself a powerful automated reporting mechanism.

3. **Web Scraping to Excel**: The ability to retrieve data directly from the web to an Excel sheet is an invaluable tool. Python's libraries such as Beautiful Soup and Scrapy excel in executing complex web scraping tasks. So, if your job entails frequent web scraping for data compilation in Excel, Python can streamline this so effectively, you may never manually scrape data again!

4. **Automated Emailing**: If regularly sending out emails that incorporate Excel attachments or data is a part of your professional life, Python's smtplib library offers you relief. It enables automatic sending of email notifications, status updates, and even attachments, reducing manual intervention to practically zero.

5. **Task Scheduling**: Remember, Python doesn't just automate tasks; it can automate when these tasks should happen too. Whether you need a report generated every Friday at 3 p.m. or web scraping to happen every month's end, Python's libraries such as schedule and celery allow for scheduling these tasks efficiently.

6. **Statistical Analysis and Machine Learning**: Excel

somewhat struggles when it comes to advanced statistical analysis and is a non-starter for machine learning. Python, with pandas for advanced statistics and scikit-learn for machine learning, can extend Excel's capabilities in these areas.

These examples only scratch the surface of what Python and Excel, working in harmony, can accomplish. If you've ever found yourself contemplating a tedious task in Excel and imagined automating it, there's a good chance Python could be your magic wand.

Armed with these insights, let's now embark on your learning journey, steadfast in our quest to judiciously harness the power of Python and Excel. Buckle in as we navigate the intricacies and amenities of these essential tools, preparing you to conquer a variety of professional challenges that lie ahead.

About Your Learning Journey

As we tread further into the annals of computational efficiency, it's only fitting to provide deeper insights into the journey you are about to undertake by converging Python's programmatic genius with Excel's user-friendly interface. Sit tight, as we delve deep into the myriad of challenges and victories that lie ahead.

Harnessing information to work in our favour requires a certain grit and patience, a thirst to overcome restrictions and limitations. This journey is about empowering and equipping you with the skills to bridge the gap between issues and results. This book isn't merely a series of coding instructions. Instead, it seeks to inculcate a profound understanding of the inner workings, underlying principles, and direct application of Python and Excel in the vast arena of real-world situations.

You might be wondering about the prerequisites for embarking on this journey. Let us assure you, this journey requires no fancy degrees or complex prerequisites, apart from your desire to learn. The idea is to render labels like 'beginner' or 'expert' as inconsequential. The real goal is to provide you with a comprehensive understanding of the symbiotic relationship between Python and Excel. Whether it's finance or research, marketing or academics, you'll learn to tackle tasks with amplified efficiency and finesse.

This book has been designed to imitate a voyage. Starting from the disembarking at 'Python and Excel Harbour', heading towards the islands of installing Python, setting up Excel, understanding their fundamental concepts, we eventually navigate to the deeper sea of complex Python for Excel interfaces and advanced data analysis. As we journey further, we explore the realms of Data Cleaning and reach the pinnacle with automating Excel tasks using Python. Finally, we close with the grand finale where we implement all that we've learned in practical real-world projects. As a bonus, we'd leave you with ample resources for continued learning and ways to connect with the myriad Python and Excel communities around the world.

This odyssey is as much about understanding the theories as it's about getting your hands dirty by delving into the code. Throughout, you'll find numerous Python coding examples, specific to Excel tasks, complemented by guided hands-on exercises to cement your understanding. These are carefully curated to ensure you get to experience a variety of commonly encountered scenarios.

Remember, as we embark on this journey, to cultivate a mindset of curiosity and exploration. Acquiring new knowledge can be challenging at times, but true mastery comes from perseverance and ceaseless practice.

Sit back as we dip our oars in and begin to row through the complexities and quirks of Python and Excel. This boat is setting sail. Welcome aboard on this enlightening journey, packed with a plethora of opportunities for gaining new insights and expanding your horizons. Get ready to brace the waves and celebrate the victories that inevitably lie ahead in this remarkable synergy called Python and Excel.

CHAPTER 2:
SETTING-UP YOUR DEVELOPMENT ENVIRONMENT

Installing Python

Embrace the onset of a captivating adventure as we make our first move: installing Python, the programming language that powers many exciting applications from web development to artificial intelligence, and now, our quest to master Excel operations at an unprecedented scale.

Python's syntax is designed to be clean and straightforward, making it a viable choice across various sectors. Installing Python is thus an indispensable step towards harnessing its power, underpinning our expedition and beyond. Don't let the term 'installation' daunt you - the following is a meticulously designed guide to facilitate a smooth Python installation process.

Starting off, we need to fetch the most updated Python version suitable for your operating system from the Python official website. A quick visit to their downloads page presents options for different operating systems - Windows, MacOS, and Linux. Select the option congruent with your Operating System. Hit

'Download Python' and the download should initiate promptly.

Following the successful download, navigate to your 'Download' folder to locate the installation file. Double clicking the file will initiate the Python installation window. At this juncture, be certain to check the little box at the bottom ensuring the PATH is set correctly. This step is crucial as it adds Python to the environmental variables, allowing you to execute Python from any command-line interface, be it Terminal on Mac or Command Prompt on Windows.

Next, select the 'Customize Installation' option. Unless you're constrained by space, it is favourable to let Python be installed in its default directory. To implement Python in conjunction with Excel commands, be sure to tick all optional features before proceeding.

Ensure that the 'Install for all users' checkbox is ticked and leave the rest of the settings at their defaults. Now go ahead and click on the 'Install Now' button. Python's installer will take a few moments to carry out the installation process.

Once completed, you'll see an 'Installation Successful' message. It's like opening the door to an avant-garde world of problem-solving allure. Hassle-free and quick, isn't it?

At this point, let's verify the installation by opening your command-line interface. Simply type in 'python --version' and press enter. If the installation was a success, this command should return the version of Python you've installed.

The installation of Python brings us one step closer to our destination: broadening our proficiency in Excel operations. But this is merely the beginning - we've only grazed the exterior of what's possible with Python. And soon, we'll delve deeper into unchartered realms where Excel and Python not only co-exist, but thrive in symbiotic harmony.

Whether you are embarking on this journey as an absolute neophyte or as someone already possessing refined programming prowess, the objective remains the same: utilising Python as a potent tool to push Excel's boundaries.

So, as we move forward in this narrative of code and cells, let's relish every moment of the process of installing Python - the initial, crucial leap towards unveiling the magic integration of Python and Excel!

Excel Read

Striding forth into the realm of efficiency, let's now ensure that Excel is armed and ready to bathe in the seamless interaction with Python. Entwining Excel and Python produces a powerful toolkit capable of rising to the challenges of almost any data analysis project. Here's how to make sure your Excel is primed for this pioneering venture.

To begin, we must ensure we're running the most up-to-date version of Microsoft Excel. Microsoft is known for pushing out constant updates: from bug fixes and security patches to the introduction of new features and enhancements. Running an outdated version can lead to compatibility issues, inefficient workflows, and reduced performance.

To upgrade your Excel version, visit your Office 365 portal or the Microsoft Office website. From there, navigate to the 'Update Options' dropdown and select 'Update Now'. Your system should then download the latest version of Excel and perform the upgrade. Once you've accomplished this, relaunch Excel and verify you are operating on the current version.

Next, let's gear our attention towards installing the Microsoft Office Developer Tools. This add-in eases the interaction between Excel and Python. To install, you'll need to navigate to 'File > Options > Customize Ribbon' inside Excel. Here, you'll see the Developer checkbox. Tick it and hit OK to enable the Developer tab studded with a range of new options for developers and seasoned users alike.

The Developer Tools provide direct ways to connect Excel with Python utilizing VBA (Visual Basic for Applications), permitting the use of Python scripts within Excel. Pro-tip: it's advisable to become conversant with the features of the Developer tab, as we'll find ourselves returning here regularly throughout our journey.

Additional useful Excel settings include auto-saving and auto-recovery - lifelines for when your system crashes or if Excel is forced to close unexpectedly. Recouping unsaved data is as easy as navigating to 'File > Options > Save', and enabling 'Save AutoRecover information every X minutes', with X denoting the frequency at which you desire Excel to autosave your work. Activating such settings can save hours of work and minimizes the risk of data loss.

Furthermore, explore Excel's Trust Center, a platform to manage security settings for macros, ActiveX controls, and add-ins. Located under 'File > Options > Trust Center > Trust Center Settings', you're given autonomy over what content is permitted to run on Excel.

Preparing your Excel environment introduces you to a series

of tools and settings to confer harmony between Python and Excel. While the process may seem labyrinthine, its value is unparalleled, guaranteeing a sturdy foundation on which to engage further.

Having our Excel installation spruced up is akin to prepping the canvas before the actual painting takes place. With Excel and Python both installed and eager, they now lay in anticipation of their spectacular ensemble, revealing a riveting narrative of automation hitherto unimagined. Stay tuned as we unbiasedly dive into this intriguing synthesis, embracing it with welcoming arms and avid minds alike.

Python Libraries for Excel

Heralding the union of Excel and Python, we find ourselves amidst the core aspects of our data-driven narrative: Python libraries for Excel. Python libraries enhance the native capabilities of Python, extending the palette of tools for us to paint our data masterpiece. For the context of interfacing with Excel, an array of pertinent libraries comes to fore.

First on this list is *pandas*. Pandas numb the barriers between Python and Excel, its DataFrame functioning as a flexible, yet powerful, data structure for reading and writing Excel files. Through pandas, we can read and write Excel files (`.xls`, `.xlsx`) with nuanced control - a paradigm shift of magnitude for keen data astronauts like us. Keeping pandas up-to-date is essential. To do this, run `pip install pandas --upgrade` in your Python environment to ensure you're utilizing the latest enhancements pandas has to offer.

Taking advantage of pandas' capabilities requires the installation of two dependencies namely - *xlrd* and *openpyxl*.

Xlrd is required to read data and format information from older Excel files(`.xls`) whereas openpyxl is utilized for reading and writing newer Excel files(`.xlsx`). To install, execute `pip install xlrd openpyxl` in your Python environment.

Next on our lead of libraries is *xlwings*, an awe-inspiring tool that acts as a conduit between Excel and Python. Xlwings allows us to coalesce the capabilities of Python and Excel, leveraging the strengths of both. It enables us to utilize Python scripts and packages directly within Excel, thereby unlocking a world of opportunities, including automating Excel tasks, crafting Excel functions, manipulating Excel files, and interactive debugging. To install xlwings, use `pip install xlwings` in your Python environment.

Making things even more tantalizing is *pywin32*, a Python library that provides an API to interact with Microsoft Windows applications. This library enables running Python scripts from VBA (Visual Basic for Applications), making Excel interact directly with Python. To install pywin32, run `pip install pywin32`.

The final noteworthy stop on our Python library roadshow is *xlsxwriter*, proficient in creating Excel files from scratch with an impressive range of features. This includes writing numbers, text, formatting cells, manipulating columns and rows, creating charts, inserting images, and more. With xlsxwriter, we gain a fine-grained control to make Excel dance to our Python tunes. Install xlsxwriter using `pip install xlsxwriter`.

These Python libraries – pandas, xlrd, openpyxl, xlwings, pywin32, and xlsxwriter – form the pillars of our interaction between Python and Excel. By shifting the tectonic plates of data analysis, they promise to lend you the tools to unearth insightful revelations lying beneath the realms of raw data.

With an armor-wrought with such potent libraries, we're armed to the teeth to wage against the most convoluted data challenges and emerge victorious. Are you ready for the conquest? Let's march forward and embrace the power these Python libraries harbour. Pave the way to an embellished portfolio of Excel tasks, performed not manually, but autonomously – a feat only Python can bestow.

Testing Your Setup

Every grand tour requires a test drive; every grand symphony, a rehearsal. And so, our dance with Python and Excel should also pass muster wayfarer's strumming. To ensure you're setup for the journey we're about to embark on, let's put to test our Python and Excel setup, checking the integrity of our newly installed libraries and ensuring their seamless functionality.

Our first test is to substantiate the successful installation of pandas, a central player in our data-driven narrative. Fret not, for this test is surprisingly simple. Commence by launching your Python environment and enter `import pandas as pd`. If this command runs without errors and you're greeted with a fresh line ready for your command, rejoice! The pandas are indeed in attendance, ready to march on your command.

Next, we move to confirm the attendance of our friendly companions, xlrd and openpyxl, the drivers behind pandas' ability to read and write Excel files. To do this, type `import xlrd` and `import openpyxl` in your Python environment. The silent compliance of Python is the salute we seek, signaling us to move ahead.

With pandas and its drivers working, let's invite to the stage *xlwings*. Raising an invocation `import xlwings as xw` should soar smoothly without any hitches. If Python complies solemnly, our wings are indeed strong and ready for flight, prepared to fly over the vast landscapes of Excel.

Our tour of confirmations takes us next to pywin32. This tool working in indelible harmony with Excel and Python is central to our epic tale. Run `import win32com.client` in your Python environment. Here again, our watchword is silence - Python's silence confirms the successful invocation of pywin32.

Finally, we're onto the last act of our play - confirming the installation of xlsxwriter. By running `import xlsxwriter`, we seek Python's silent endorsement, confirming we're ready to paint the town red (or any other color xlsxwriter allows!).

And there you have it! A dive into the pool of Python libraries, a relay across installation commands, and a dash to check if all's well. If the Python environment gracefully accepted all your import statements, then indeed, all's well! This signifies a solid foundation, and we're ready for elegant pirouettes and complex choreography of data that lies ahead.

But wait! What if Python decided to shed a tear or two in the form of errors? It's an indication of turbulent signs. If Python raises an ImportError, it means the mentioned library isn't accessible. Double-check your installation steps and ensure the libraries are installed in the correct Python environment.

Once you've addressed the issue, rinse and repeat the testing process. Recall, the best summits are reached not by chance, but by meticulous preparation. Let's blaze the trail across the highlands of Excel, under the banner of Python, hand-in-hand with these fantastically capable libraries. We are, after all, poets of data, and we've got a grand sonnet to compose!

Troubleshooting & Tips

There are journeys where the course is as smooth as silk, and there are those that challenge us with every mile covered. Our venture into the world of Python and Excel will, indeed, dish out its own flavor of trials. But as the guardians of your exploration, we won't let you lose your way. So, let's delve into some common issues you may encounter, and how to navigate through these occasional stumbles on the path of programming.

Let's start with package installation errors. 'Permission Denied' or 'Could not install packages due to Environment Error' are common bane of Python enthusiasts. These could be due to a myriad of factors - sometimes, it's an incompatible Python environment, or you're trying to install in a non-writable directory. There's a quite ingenious way around these hurdles! Try installing using ` --user ` while using pip to bypass permission issues. For example, it would look something like, ` pip install --user pandas `.

Ah, what's that? Encountered 'network-related' errors? Fear not. Sometimes, Python's pip can be a little touchy about internet connectivity. Recheck your internet connection and try running the command again. Persistent pest? Pip mirrors can work wonders here. These are alternative download sites we can point pip towards.

Stepped into ImportError quicksand, have we? Fret not! If Python raises an ImportError, it means it couldn't find your library. It's time to confirm the library's presence and the environment it resides in. Is it possible that the library got installed in a different Python environment by mistake? A little bit of an investigation using `pip list` will list all installed packages in your active Python environment. Stick around for a couple minutes, acquaint yourself with the list, and spot our library guests.

Remember, Python can be quite the rigorous doorman. If an incorrect case is used - let's say openpyxl is called as openPYxl, Python is likely to slam the door shut, resulting in an ImportError. Always use the correct case - our eccentric Python doorman demands it!

Python slurring its speech with a SyntaxError, is it? Keep a keen eye on punctuation - a forgotten colon, an accidental indentation, a missing bracket - these common 'typos' are often the culprits.

Looking for libraries can be a tiresome chore for Python, resulting in ModuleNotFoundError if it doesn't find what it's looking for. With paths to negotiate and environment variables to mine, even Python could do with some guidance. Try using a full path in your import statement or add the path to the Python library into your environment variables.

These are just a few of the conundrums you might encounter on your scripting journey. When it comes to troubleshooting, keep two things close to heart - error messages are your map, and Google, your trusty compass. A little perseverance, and who knows, you might stumble into even more remarkable advents than you initially intended! After all, we learn little from victory, much from defeat. Now, back to our expedition - with Python and Excel waiting, we have worlds to conquer!

CHAPTER 3:
PYTHON BASICS

Understanding Syntax

Embarking on our second voyage to the heart of Python, we find ourselves at the threshold of the land of syntax. Here we will unlock the secrets of Python's complex ecosystem, tracing the paths of its logic, trellising its expressions, and understanding how it manipulates the data that ripples through its veins.

Python's syntax is an austere landscape, belied by a simplicity that feels almost antithetical to its depths. Its strength lies in its ability to articulate complex algorithms with an economy of words. No excessive punctuation to muddy the clarity of your thought, only a clean canvas to paint your data-driven masterpieces.

The first landmarks in this expedition into Pythonic syntax are these simple yet powerful words: print, input, def, return, for, while, if, else, elif. They guide the program, transforming user inputs into desired outputs and handling the necessary conditions and loops to create multifaceted applications.

For instance, `print()` is your messenger, the bridge between your program and the world outside. It shares your revelations and discoveries, providing insights into a program's machinations. To use it, simply i.e `print("Hello, World!")`, and it faithfully echoes your words to the console.

Next comes `input()`, Python's ears that absorb user inputs. Like a patient listener, it takes a string input, and waits for a user's response. Through it, your program can interact, engage and dynamically adapt to the outside world. Try `name = input("What's your name? ")`, and Python saves the user's response in the 'name' variable. Is not this dialogue a magnificent orchestra between user and machine?

We now venture deeper into Python's jungle of syntax. Functions, a set of reusable code that performs a specific task, are denoted by `def()`. They allow coders to compress their logic, extracting utilities and abstracting complexity. In its simplest form, it looks as `def name_of_func():`. It is waiting, eager to encapsulate your unique instructions and commands.

To transfer data from a function, we employ `return`. An altruistic operator, it passes along the result of a function to other parts of your program. It is `return` that ensures your functions aren't isolated bubbles, but rather cogs in a connected machine that exchange data in beautiful harmony.

Next, we encounter conditional and looping operators - `if`, `else`, `elif`, `for`, `while`. These are the traffic signals of Python, orchestrating the flow of information. An `if` statement serves as the decision-maker, evaluating conditions and determining the direction of your code. Coupled with the `else` and `elif` statements, it allows Python to navigate the numerous possibilities and exceptions that may arise.

Loops, denoted by `for` and `while`, are like a circling hawk repeatedly performing the same action over a collection of items or until a condition is met. They are the torchbearers of Python's emphasis on automation, eradicating the need for repetitive commands and keeping your code clean and efficient.

Understanding Python's syntax illuminates the path that data traverses in a program, illuminating the chain of reasoning, loops, conditions and functions. With this knowledge you are ready to create, to imagine, to weave together intricate tapestries of algorithms with Python mastery. Now go forth, explorer, and unravel the algorithmic marvels that await you.

Variables and Data Types

Having crossed the terrain of Python syntax, we now stand at the foothills of the next significant zone - the realm where variables and data types reside. Like narrators of a spirited tale, variables store, transform, and regale with data, while data types are the generational styles employed by these variables, shaping the way they interact with, manipulate, and represent data.

In Python, a variable is a named area in the memory where data is stored. Here, it waits, poised to be transformed, manipulated, published, all based on your program's whims. Our data's custodian, it takes on an evocative form - a name of your choosing. By assigning a value, the variable comes to life, it may seem like `x = 10` or `username = 'sam123'`. From that moment, it becomes the embodiment of assigned data propelled by your narrative.

A fascinating aspect of Python is that it's dynamically typed, hence the script would be akin to an open-ended dialogue, replete with twists and possibilities. Unlike other rigorous and unchanging chronicles, Python's variables can transmute - an integer to a string, a float to a boolean, and so forth, all depending on the role our narrative requires them to play.

The data can take on several masks within Python - the Boolean, which like a binary puzzle box, dwells entirely in the world of True and False. The Numeric, a broad class that further branches into integers, floating point numbers, and complex numbers, each with their own story. When the Numeric met a sequence of characters, the String type was born, a more sophisticated and elaborate entity. Complementing these are the Lists and Tuples, versatile types that are capable of storing a wide scope of data types in an ordered sequence. And finally, the Dictionaries, that transform data into a game of keys and corresponding values.

Let us look at some practical examples to further illuminate these concepts. A Boolean can be represented as `isTrue = True` or `isFalse = False`. Numeric types are even simpler, a straightforward `customerAge = 25` or `purchaseAmount = 19.99`. Strings are a little more theatrical, such as `customerName = "Sam Walton"`. Lists are an ensemble cast, storing different variable types like `shoppingList = ['Apples', 12, 'Bananas', 6]`. And the Dictionaries play a twin act assigning values to keys, such as `customerRecord = {'Name': 'Sam', 'Age': 25}`.

Answering the clarion call to command the data ocean with deftness, Python endeavors to equip the programmer with a vast armory of data types. Grasping these data types and understanding their connotations, their relationships with each other, and their ability to encapsulate real-world scenarios, you breathe life into your code, thereby realizing Python's true capabilities. Well-versed in this linguistics of data, we're prepared now to journey deeper, to form expressions and undertake operations with these variables – an encounter we shall undertake with anticipation. So, let's gather these learnings, excel further and embark on the Python narrative, starting at none other than Python operations.

Basic Operations

Voyaging ahead in our Python odyssey, we encounter a new territory marked by the buzz of computational activity. This realm is known for Basic Operations - the building blocks of any code. Imagine these operations as the swift currents that guide the course of data in the expansive sea of Python.

Immersed in basic operations, our variables and data types find themselves tumbling in the thrill of arithmetical equations, comparisons, and logical propositions. These basic operations supply our Python code with the ability to perform tasks, solve problems, and make decisions, all adding towards the flexibility and power our Python programs can harness.

We begin our exploration with mathematical operations, the ones you might recollect from your school years with a newfound appreciation. Python streamlines addition (`+`), subtraction (`-`), multiplication (`*`), division (`/`), and even the modulus (`%`) which finds the remainder in division operations. A useful operator called floor division (`//`), a division operation where the decimal part of the result is discarded, reiterates Python's practical narrative. Additionally, Python dabbles in exponents too, using the power operator (`**`).

To paint a more vivid portrait, consider this example – let's define two variables, `x = 7` and `y = 3`. We can seamlessly perform these operations: `x+y` results in `10`, `x-y` in `4`, `x*y` in `21`, `x/y` gets us `2.33`, `x%y` gives `1`, `x//y` shows `2` and `x**y` manifests `343`.

Yet, numbers alone don't shape our Python tale. Here, variables of distinct data types engage in comparisons, mirroring reality, assessing equality (`==`), inequality (`!=`), less than (`<`), more than (`>`), less than or equal to (`<=`), and more than or equal to (`>=`). Take for instance `a = 'apple`` and `b = 'banana'`; in Python, `a > b` returns False, since in ASCII, apple precedes banana.

Furthermore, we traverse the threshold where our Python script begins to depict complex narratives, one where it emulates human decision-making. The logical operators `and`, `or`, and `not` wedge themselves between these variables and examine whether the statements are True or False. If `p = True` and `q = False`, operations like `p and q` returns False, `p or q` returns True, and `not p` returns False.

Our endeavours further demonstrate that these product operations between our variables aren't merely interactions but form the pathways enabling data to flow from one part of the program to another. As the Python narrative advances, these basic operations morph into more sophisticated functions, substantiating Python's status as the unabridged language of computing.

As we dock at the shore of this operational realm, we find ourselves better programmers, capable of making our Python programs think, assess, calculate and most importantly, decide. The journey doesn't end here, though. We have uncovered the power of operations but still have the structures that control these operations left to explore — a Python adventure we shall embark on in our ensuing journey into Control Structures.

Control Structures

Having threaded through the sands of Basic Operations, we land ashore the island of Control Structures, ready to confront a slightly more challenging yet exciting adventure. This mysterious landscape stands tall with the potent constructs that navigate the course of data flowing in our Python programs, enabling them to be more responsive, rational and flexible.

Welcome to the dynamic world of Control Structures, where conditional statements, looping structures, and control statements intertwine, forming the code's logic. Think of Control Structures as the invisible puppet masters, skillfully pulling the strings, commanding the scene, and demanding from the code to perform particular tasks under specific circumstances.

Carved from the heart of Python, conditional statements form the first pillar of Control Structures. Through the `if`, `elif`, and `else` keywords, Python scripts get outfitted with the ability to test conditions and make decisions. An analogy akin to life's important decisions illustrates their operations. If the condition is met, a specific block of code gets executed – a pathway triggered only when the condition evaluates as True.

Let's take a Pythonic gaze into a simple control structure:
```python
if x > y:
    print('x is greater')
elif x < y:
    print('y is greater')
```

else:

    print('x and y are equal')
` ` `

Whence `x` and `y` are defined variables, the script takes an assessment, compares, and decides, subsequently printing the outcome corresponding to the truth of the evaluated condition.

The second pillar, looping structures, pioneered by the `for` and `while` loops, is similar to a hamster's wheel. It commands repetitive execution of a code block—yet, more efficiently, without tirelessly re-writing the code. With a specified condition, the `for` loop iterates over a sequence, whereas the `while` continues until the condition remains True. These loops are like patient fishers, casting their net over and over until a plentiful catch is secured.

Consider a basic `for` loop:
` ` `python
for i in range(10):

    print(i)
` ` `

The loop interacts with the range function to print numbers 0-9, iterating the process until the range is exhausted– a glimpse of the diligent `for` loop at work.

Last in line, but equally important in contributory value, are the control statements—the `break`, `continue`, and `pass` commands. These are Python's powerful commando troops deployed to control the flow of loops. `break` commands the loop to terminate immediately, `continue` skips the rest of the loop for the current iteration and proceeds to the next, while `pass` plays a placeholder role for future code, ensuring no errors occur.

As daunting as Control Structures may initially seem, they are the brain and nerve of Python programs. By calculating conditions, perpetuating tasks, and controlling flow, they develop Python into a potent, problem-solving language. So here we stand, in awe of Control Structures, heads held high, fingers on the keyboard, ready to continue sailing through our thrilling journey in Python.

Functions in Python

As we push through the dense, symbolic forests of Python, we abruptly encounter the magical realm of Functions, an essential piece of the Python puzzle. This mystifying territory beckons us with the enchantment of cutting code repetition, enhancing code readability, and escalating scalability - a trinity of sorts that empower Python's efficiency.

Functions are entities in Python that encapsulate reusable pieces of code which can be executed whenever called upon. This group of related statements that performs a specific task acts like a miniature independent program within the larger context of Python coding. While they may initially seem bewildering, Functions are truly your best companions in crafting an efficient Python program. Let's dive in!

The Python language provides built-in functions such as print(), len(), etc., but Python doesn't stop there. It also proffers the opportunity to create your own custom functions, or as Python likes to call them, the user-defined functions.

User-defined functions formulation primarily relies on two components; the `def` keyword, followed by the function name and parentheses `()`. Within these parentheses, one can spool arguments pertinent to the function. This frame is followed by a colon `:` commencing block indentation, under which the function's operation is defined. Finally, to garner the function's final outcome, the statement `return [expression]` is often used, signposting the function's finale.

Consider the following example:

```python
def hello_world():
    return "Hello, World!"
print(hello_world())
```

This simple function, when called, returns the string "Hello, World!", a candid showcase of a user-defined function in action.

Python's ticket to sophistication is its ability to harness parameters in functions. Much like how our DNA makes us unique, parameters allow functions to process unique data and furnish individualistic results each time they are called. It is the freedom to insert parameters while calling a function that makes functions dynamic.

Take a look at the following function with parameters:

```python
def greet_me(name):
    return "Hello, " + name + "!"
print(greet_me("Alice"))
```

Here, 'Alice' is passed into the function as an argument, leading to a personalized greeting for Alice.

Python also extends its project to make room for special types of functions, such as Lambda, or anonymous functions. The term 'anonymous' alludes to these functions being declared with no name. Lambda functions are essentially small, simple, temporary functions making one-time use-case scenarios more efficient.

Here's Lambda function at work:

```python
double = lambda x: x * 2
print(double(5))
```

This Lambda function takes a number 'x', multiplies it by 2, and returns the result. When called with 5 as an argument, it blithely returns 10.

In the spellbinding realm of Python, Functions are the charming wizards - magical and efficient, ready to perform and enchant. They are the alluring crochet to Python's tapestry, a testament to Python's strive for code efficiency, readability and scalability. As we explore more of this intriguing territory, let us allow this wizardry to draw us into the mesmerizing depths of Python.

CHAPTER 4: EXCEL ESSENTIALS

Spreadsheet Basics

Embarking on a voyage through the concept of spreadsheets, we encounter our next stop - the basics of Excel. Transposed neatly on the intersection of rows and columns, this electronic checkboard within the Microsoft Office Suite is a favourite among data enthusiasts across the globe. Excel offers a platform to effortlessly manage, analyse, and visualise a whole gamut of data. From simple number crunching to performing complex data analysis tasks, Microsoft Excel serves a variety of roles in today's data-driven world.

A quintessential Excel spreadsheet harbours cells. Cells are the primary building blocks of an Excel sheet, taking the shape of individual boxes within the grid. Every cell references a unique intersection of a row and column, and is involved in storing, manipulating and displaying data.

While rows in Excel are marked numerically from 1 onwards, Excel marks columns alphabetically from A to Z, then from AA to AZ, and so on, up to XFD in the latest versions of Excel. This layout breeds an intuitive structure to store and organise data effectively, fielding a seamless data management experience.

Excel also provides an ample supply of formulas and built-in functions to perform automatic calculations on data. Basic mathematical operations such as addition (+), subtraction (-), multiplication (*), and division (/) are all game on Excel. As an example, entering "=5+5" into a cell would result in "10."

Consider the following example where cells A1 and A2 contain the numbers 5 and 2, respectively:

```excel
Cell B1: =A1+A2
```

After you hit enter, Excel would compute and display the result "7" in cell B1. This is an autocalculation Excel performs using cell references and mathematical operations.

For information larger than a cell, Excel hands us the baton to use range. A range in Excel is a collection of two or more cells that you manage collectively rather than individually. Defined by the references of the top left and bottom right cell separated by a colon, ranges in Excel play a pivotal role when dealing with masses of data.

Excel charts are another valuable tool in Excel's arsenal. Casting quantitative data into a visual presentation not only entices the audience but also sheds light on trends and patterns hidden in raw numbers. Excel provides a vast variety of chart types, such as line, column, bar, pie, scatter plot, and many more. Each tailors to different data representation needs, breathing life into tedious number stacks.

Taking the first row as column headers, let's create a bar chart, where the first column represents the category and the second as data value. Excel intuitively categorises the 'categories' on the X-axis and displays the 'data values' vertically forming bars on the Y-axis. The height of these bars embodies the magnitude of the 'data value.'

This encapsulates the basics of spreadsheets, enveloped in the charm of Excel. As we journey through real-world applications and adroit Excel techniques, this foundational knowledge forges an essential stepping stone to a deeper understanding of Excel's robust capabilities in handling and processing data.

Formulas and Functions

Setting sail towards Excel's immense ocean of capabilities, we encounter our next stop - formulas and functions. Excel, at first glance, might appear to be a simple grid of cells, waiting to be filled with static data. But underneath it all, Excel is a robust ecosystem supporting an amplifying cycle of dynamic interaction of operations. In this vein, two of the powerful components ndeeded to unlock this dynamic potential are 'formulas' and 'functions.'

Excel's 'formula' is the tool that provides the ability to perform calculations on a set of data. Each formula in Excel begins with an equal sign (=), followed by a series of operators (like +, -, *, or /) and cell references. A simple formula could look as follows:

```excel
Cell B3: =B1+B2
```

Upon entering, Excel evaluates the formula, add numbers in cells B1 and B2, and display the result in cell B3. You can modify a formula by altering the numbers in the referenced cells or by modifying the formula itself. Excel then automatically recalculates the result highlighting the dynamic nature of its computational capacity.

However, Excel doesn't stop here. It offers a cornucopia of pre-defined 'functions'. Think of a function as a professionally designed, pre-packaged formula. Excel functions range from simple operations, like SUM or AVERAGE, that save you effort in writing the formulas yourself, to complex tools, like INDEX-MATCH or VLOOKUP, that are powerful enough to manage, look-up and cross-reference large sets of data. By using Excel functions, you can efficiently crunch numbers, perform statistical analyses, and even build complex financial models.

For example, consider a range of numbers in cells A1 to A5. Instead of adding each cell separately, the SUM function can calculate a total while accommodating changes in the data set over time. The function would look like this:

```excel
Cell A6: =SUM(A1:A5)
```

Such dynamic functions are not limited to numerical data; text or string-based functions like CONCATENATE or LEFT, RIGHT and MID, also add to the versatility of Excel. For instance, if you want to join (or concatenate) the two texts in cell A1 and B1, you would use:

```excel
```

Cell C1: =CONCATENATE(A1, " ", B1)
```
` ` `
```

This outputs a single text string in cell C1 with the contents of A1 and B1 separated by a space.

Along with these, Excel offers sophisticated logical functions like IF, hypotheses testing functions like T.TEST, and even date and time manipulative functions like NOW and DAY. All these functions play an instrumental role in boosting Excel's computational prowess and adding versatility to data management.

In the latticework of Excel, where each cell waits to hold a nugget of information, formulas and functions are the tools, the magic wands that transform, manipulate and govern the logic of data interaction. Guided by these, users embarking on their Excel Odyssey now unravel and leverage the dynamic capabilities of Excel with facility and confidence.

Creating Charts and Graphs

After navigating numerical torrents and character rivers in Excel with formulas and functions, it's time to give a visual representation to this sea of information. A picture, they say, is worth a thousand words, and when it comes to data comprehension, a good graph trumps rows of numbers. Therefore, the next phase of our exploration focuses on mastering the art of snapshot storytelling with Excel: It's now time to create charts and graphs.

The core of a spreadsheet is colossal facts and figures. Inspecting such information may prove daunting, often hiding critical patterns and correlations. However, unfolding the same data through charts and graphs unravels a narrative, exposing abstract patterns and unseen correlations, while relaying its story in a precise, visually compelling format that accelerates data comprehension.

Excel presents a multitude of chart options, each equipped to tell a unique data story. Whether you're tracking sales trends over time with a Line Chart, comparing market shares with a Pie Chart, examining distribution with a Histogram, or exploring correlations with a Scatter Plot, Excel charts cater to every narrative. Here's how to breathe life into your data by transforming it into a chart:

1. Click and drag to select the range of cells containing data you'd like to chart.

2. Navigate to the 'Insert' tab, and select a chart type from 'Charts' group. For instance, if you wish to create a Line Chart:

```excel
Excel Command: Insert > Line Chart > Line
```

3. After selecting a chart, Excel will generate it based on your data and put it in your worksheet. You can further customise your chart using chart tools.

Excel also caters to the complexity and depth of data visualisation through its multi-faceted function - the Combo Chart. This unique chart allows the combination of two or more chart types into one, handling different data series that may require distinct chart types.

But what if you want to emphasize the highs and lows, or the progress towards a specific target? Excel got you covered. Sparklines are mini-charts placed in single cells, providing a clear and compact visual representation of your data. You can inset a sparkline by:

```excel
Excel Command: Insert > Sparklines > Line
```

When dealing with a copious amount of data, a PivotChart serves as a powerful tool, allowing you to create dynamic graphics that can be easily manipulated and updated, without programming or complex formulas. The user-friendly visual interface let you move fields around, to create an interactive chart that highlights the necessary data points and patterns.

In this colourful realm of Excel, static numbers become dynamic visuals, piecing together a beautiful mosaic of information. Charting in Excel is not just about making data more digestible; it's about expressing the narrative that grapples this data, it's about transforming static numbers into an engaging, relatable story. Watch as Excel morphs from a spreadsheet tool into a canvas, and let's continue painting the data story in the subsequent sections.

Managing Data with Excel

Mastering Microsoft Excel entails dexterity beyond making spreadsheets, applying formulas, or creating illustrative visuals. It is about taming the mammoth of data-driven insights and tackling the vast expanse of figures. Welcome to part 4.4, where we tap into the often underrated prowess of Excel - managing data.

Data, the oil of the digital age, can often appear unwieldy, dishevelled, seemingly chaotic, and growing at an alarming pace. It is brimming with valuable hidden insights, but unlocking them can be an uphill battle. Here is where Excel shines, acting like a trustworthy data shepherd, ensuring that you can manage your data herd in a structured, clean, and understandable way.

An elaborate Excel workbook can mirror a mini-database; hence, learning a few key tools related to data management can change the game. Excel's Data Tab is the point of functioning for many crucial tasks related to data management. Let's explore some of them:

Data Sorting

Sorting data is a fundamental task in data management. It makes data more comprehendible and subsequently increases processing speed. Excel supports single-column sorts (i.e., sorting by one column) and multi-column sorts (i.e., sorting by more than one column).

To sort in Excel:
```excel
Excel Command: Data > Sort & Filter > Sort A to Z or Sort Z to A
```

Data Filtering

Filtering, a method for temporarily hiding unwanted data, is a useful feature when you're dealing with vast datasets. It lets you focus on specific subsets of your data without eliminating the potential significance of other columns or rows.

To filter in Excel:

```excel
Excel Command: Data > Sort & Filter > Filter
```

Data Validation

Data validation is a marvellous tool to ensure the accuracy and consistency of the data entered into your spreadsheet. It can restrict what type of data gets entered into a cell, eliminating future inconsistencies or errors.

To set up data validation:

```excel
Excel Command: Data > Data Tools > Data Validation
```

Removing Duplicates

Excel provides the option of easily removing duplicate rows. Often essential for data cleaning, this function proves transformative in paring down your data to the unique values you may need to analyse.

To remove duplicates:

```excel
Excel Command: Data > Data Tools > Remove Duplicates
```

Text to Columns

A lot of raw data comes in a less than ideal format. Excel's `Text to Columns` feature allows you to split the contents of cells based on a delimiter or fixed width.

```excel
Excel Command: Data > Data Tools > Text to Columns
```

Out of crunchy numbers, big data and quick functions, Excel emerges as your key to manoeuvre through an ocean of data. Data management in Excel takes dull rows and columns and converts them into illuminating and significant metrics, enabling you make accurate inferences, informed decisions and uncover valuable insights. Unleash your data wizardry with Excel - make the data dance to your tunes. And as you savour the power of this instrument in managing data, let's leap onto the next step to unlock the advanced features of Excel.

Advanced Excel Features

In the realms of Excel, the known is a haven for the amateur while the unknown attracts the curious and the adventurous. In an expansive landscape guarded by grids and ruled by functions, let's unfold a chapter where the magic happens - Advanced Excel Features. It's here at the confluence where comfort meets complexity, ensuring even seasoned Excel users discover new terrain and tools to conquer.

Unleashing Excel's fundamentals is just the beginning. To become an Excel maestro requires exploring the abyss beyond comfort, diving into functionalities that are invariably time-saving and remarkably efficient. So, buckle up and get ready to embark into the deeper layers of Excel's world where advanced functions, pivots, scenarios, form controls, macros and many more features reign supreme.

Advanced Functions

Nosier the data, higher the demand for specialised functions. Excel offers advanced functions like **VLOOKUP**, **HLOOKUP**, **INDEX-MATCH** and **IF** functions to browse through data, make comparisons or complex combined conditions. Here's an example of a VLOOKUP function:

``` excel
Excel Function: =VLOOKUP(lookup_value, table_array, col_index_num, [range_lookup])
```

Pivot Tables

For dynamic data summarising, pivot tables prove to be an efficient tool. They enable slicing and dicing of data model for a profound reach to unique insights. Pivot tables sort, count, total, or average the data stored in one table or spreadsheet, displaying the results in a second table.

Scenarios

Scenarios are a part of the 'What-If' analysis toolkit. They let replicating different variables that influence a formula to project possible outcomes. It's like creating copies of the same data set with dissimilar input values.

Form Controls

Form controls add interactivity and flexibility to your Excel spreadsheets. They can make a data presentation more lucid and interactive, transform parameters, or navigate through the spreadsheets faster.

Macros

Automation is a game-changer. Excel's VBA-powered macros enable repetitive tasks to be automated, saving considerable time and reducing the possibility of human errors. Through simple to complex scripts, Macros can carry out tasks ranging from formatting cells to sending emails.

```vba
Example Macro:
Sub ColorCells()
    Range("A1:C10").Interior.Color = RGB(255, 0, 0)
End Sub
```

This macro, when run, colors the cells from A1 to C10 in red.

Always remember, the depths of Microsoft Excel are vast, and its concepts intertwined. Every function, every feature serves as a stepping-stone to the next. The marvel of Excel lies in the harmony between its facets, so dive in and seek the wisdom that the depths hold.

As we conclude our exploration of Excel's advanced capabilities, we learn that the secret to mastering Excel is the symbiotic blend of comprehension and practice. Yet we're at the start line of a marathon, for we've merely skimmed Excel's surface. The exhilarating dance between Excel's rows and columns has just begun, as we delve next into the intertwined world of Python and Excel. May our journey continue unabated, our thirst for knowledge unquenched, and our spirit ever curious.

CHAPTER 5: INTERACTING BETWEEN PYTHON AND EXCEL

Reading Excel Files with Python

Delving deeper into the synergistic communion of Python and Excel, we arrive at a crucial juncture - ingesting the skeletons of Excel data into Python's analytical framework. This so-called 'reading' of Excel files, or coaxing data out of a spreadsheet and into the Python paradigm, sets the stage for the analytical acrobatics that are to follow.

At this point, one might wonder why not sprawl out comfortably in the confines of an Excel worksheet, exploiting the in-house functionalities that suffuse it. The revelation to that query lies in Python's powerful array of data handling capacities, complemented by a repertoire of specialised library functions. The first step to leveraging these abilities is to read or load Excel data into Python, the process of which will be our earnest exploration in this section.

Use of pandas

In the pursuit of mastering reading Excel files in Python, we extend our hands to an ally - pandas. This is a potent data manipulation and analysis library in Python. An imperative part of pandas is its DataFrame structure, which lets us store and manipulate tabular data where rows denote different subjects (indexes) and columns represent various attributes.

We will utilise the read_excel method in pandas to read the contents of an Excel file.

```python
import pandas as pd

data = pd.read_excel('file.xlsx')
print(data)
```

With just two lines of code, we've managed to import an entire spreadsheet of Excel data into Python. The parameter within read_excel is the path to the Excel file you wish to read. Generally, 'file.xlsx' would be replaced with the name of your Excel file. If the file isn't located in the same directory as your Python script, you would need a full file path.

Working with multiple worksheets

Excel files often contain multiple worksheets. You can read a specific sheet by using the sheet_name parameter in the read_excel function:

```python
data = pd.read_excel('file.xlsx', sheet_name ='Sheet2')
```

```
` ` `
```

In this case, 'Sheet2' is the name of the sheet we want to read.

Discovering the openpyxl module

Another notable library in Python used for reading and writing Excel 2010 xlsx/xlsm/xltx/xltm files is openpyxl. It's robust, easy-to-use, and allows for advanced Excel operations like creating graphs, inserting images, and working with formulas.

```python
from openpyxl import load_workbook

workbook = load_workbook(filename="file.xlsx")
sheet = workbook.active
data = sheet.values
```

By reading Excel files into Python, we invite data into an environment ripe for potent manipulation, analysis, and visualization functionalities. This ability is akin to opening an ornate doorway leading to expansive possibilities of data analysis, setting the stage for our next act – writing data back into Excel.

Writing to Excel Files

Riding the tide of our data-oriented discourse, having imported data from Excel into Python, we now swim upstream: writing data back to Excel. Distilled in this unparalleled undertaking is Python's adeptness at straddling the realms of data analysis and the universal familiarity of Excel spreadsheets. Consider this: Python allows us to pierce the veil of numbers, extract revelations, permeate layers of complexities, but at the end of the day, these newly minted insights must find their way back into a spreadsheet, accessible to all. This section ascends into the exploration of such cartography of knowledge, charting the voyage of data from Python to Excel.

Employing the pandas library

Our first port of call is again pandas, which proves to be just as proficient at writing to Excel files as it is at reading from them. This is enabled by the to_excel method, which allows us to output a DataFrame to an Excel sheet:

```python
import pandas as pd

data = {'Name': ['John', 'Anna', 'Peter'],
        'Age': [34, 29, 51],
        'City': ['New York', 'Paris', 'London']}
df = pd.DataFrame(data)
df.to_excel('output.xlsx', index = False)
```

In this snippet, we first create a sample DataFrame using a dictionary. We then write this DataFrame to an Excel file named 'output.xlsx'. The argument index = False ensures that the DataFrame index is not written to the Excel file.

Writing to multiple worksheets

Often, output data isn't destined for a singular sheet, but

rather multiple sheets in the same workbook. Thankfully, pandas provides the ExcelWriter method, where we can specify different DataFrame to different sheets:

```python
with pd.ExcelWriter('output.xlsx') as writer:
    df1.to_excel(writer, sheet_name='Sheet1')
    df2.to_excel(writer, sheet_name='Sheet2')
```

Here, df1 and df2 are DataFrames that we direct to 'Sheet1' and 'Sheet2', both within the 'output.xlsx' file.

Exploring openpyxl's capabilities

Our journey doesn't halt at pandas as Python's openpyxl library graciously incorporates writing abilities as well. Use the Workbook() function to create a new workbook, and Workbook.create_sheet() for creating new sheets:

```python
from openpyxl import Workbook

book = Workbook()
sheet = book.active
sheet['A1'] = "hello"
sheet['B1'] = "world"
book.save("sample.xlsx")
```

In this example, we generate a new Excel file 'sample.xlsx'

with the cells A1 and B1 populated with the words "hello" and "world". A fresh chapter of familiarity with Python tools to navigate between the co-ordinates of Python and Excel has now been written unfolding the potential to divulge deeper into analyzing and modifying Excel files through Python, casting the spotlight next onto our next intriguing segment – manipulating Excel files.

Manipulating Excel Files

As the journey of discovery continues, we venture into uncharted territories that exist between Python and Excel, a landscape embellishing itself with every step: manipulating Excel files. Here, we dissolve the boundary line between mundanity and magic, enhancing routine spreadsheet operations with Python's power, imbuing it with finesse. The focus now shifts from a one-way traffic system - writing data to Excel - to an engaging conversation, where data is not just written but also altered, massaged, and shaped to our will.

If Python's charm lies in its simplicity, then its power is in its flexibility. After writing to an Excel file, a multitude of operations can be undertaken to manipulate the existing data. Let's unveil them.

Modifying cell contents with openpyxl

Openpyxl is the accomplice we summon to orchestrate our desired changes. Once you have identified the cell, altering its content is as simple as assigning a new value.

```python
from openpyxl import load_workbook
```

```
wb = load_workbook('sample.xlsx')
ws = wb.active
ws['B2'] = "brave new"
ws.cell(row=3, column=2, value="world")
wb.save('sample.xlsx')
```

In this scenario, the contents of a cell identified by its column and row (ws['B2'] and ws.cell(row=3, column=2)) are altered, introducing the inspirational phrase "brave new world" into the Excel file 'sample.xlsx'.

Editing row and column dimensions

Excel files are renowned for their generous provision of rows and columns that can be resized for easy viewing or aesthetics. The openpyxl library provides functions to change row heights and column widths.

```python
ws.row_dimensions[1].height = 70
ws.column_dimensions['B'].width = 20
```

Here, the height of the first row and the width of the 'B' column are altered, allowing for a customized overview of our data.

Applying and changing formatting

Every spreadsheet is a blank canvas yearning for an artistic touch, to transform data from a mere collection of numbers into a visually meaningful display. Python lets us run wild on this canvas.

```python
from openpyxl.styles import colors, Font

red_font = Font(color=colors.RED)
ws['A1'].font = red_font
wb.save('sample.xlsx')
```

In this instance, the font color of 'A1' cell is changed to red, adding a splash of color into an otherwise monochrome mise-en-scène.

Implementing Excel formulas

Imbued within Excel files is not just static data but rather a vibrant collection of formulas that represent the heart of many an analysis. Python allows us to implement these formulas.

```python
ws.cell(row=4, column=3, value="=SUM(A1:B2)")
```

In this code snippet, we employ Python to write the SUM formula into a cell.

Ultimately, Python holds the key to transforming Excel files from a mere data holding reservoir to a dynamic ecosystem. Offering irresistible power, the journey through data analysis transcends into the domain of art, painting endless possibilities for data manipulation within Excel.

Automating Tasks

As we traverse this fascinating intersection of Python and Excel, the next venture unfurls before us - the automation of Excel tasks. Casting a new light on the mundane, automation discloses efficiency, saving both time and effort - the twin towers of productivity. Like clockwork, tasks repeat, but with Python as our aid, we delegate them to the virtual realm, freeing time for strategic interventions and decision-making.

Writing Macros with Python

To many, macros are ubiquitous to Excel automation. Python brings to this automation process the magic of simplicity along with advanced functionality. Writing macros using Python accommodates a much broader range of tasks:

```python
import xlwings as xw

wb = xw.Book()
macro_vba = wb.app.macro('VBAProject.Module1.test_macro')
macro_vba('Hello World!')
wb.close()
```

In this example, we are invoking the `VBAProject.Module1.test_macro` from Excel's VBA (Visual Basic for Applications) module, using Python's `xlwings` module. This demonstrates how Python can function as an able agent to trigger macros.

Task Scheduling with Python

Beyond scripting repetitive tasks, Python also gives you the ability to schedule these tasks. Leveraging Python's `schedule` library, you can execute your automated tasks at designed intervals.

```python
import schedule
import time

def task():
    print("Task Completed!")

schedule.every(10).minutes.do(task)

while True:
    schedule.run_pending()
    time.sleep(1)
```

The code snippet above displays an elementary yet potent system where a function, `task()`, runs every 10 minutes. The function's functionality can range from data analysis to sending automated emails, limited only by the scope of your needs and imagination.

Automating Excel Reporting

Reporting is often an underappreciated warrior of decision-making. High-frequency, routine reports can be automated using Python, saving time, reducing the chances of errors and enabling timely access to information.

```python
import pandas as pd
from openpyxl import Workbook
from openpyxl.utils.dataframe import dataframe_to_rows

df = pd.read_excel('sales_data.xlsx')
df_summary = df.groupby('Product').sum()

wb = Workbook()
ws = wb.create_sheet('Summary', 0)

for i in dataframe_to_rows(df_summary, index=True, header=True):
    ws.append(i)

wb.save('sales_summary.xlsx')
```

This code helps in automatically generating a sales summary report from a raw data file. It reads the `sales_data.xlsx` file using pandas, aggregates the sales data product-wise, writes the summary into a new Excel worksheet 'Summary', and saves the file as 'sales_summary.xlsx'.

Smart Notifications

Python paves the way for smart notifications. By intercepting critical points in your automated workflows, Python scripts can be set to send emails, push notifications, or even help slack messages alerting you or your team to significant events.

```python
import smtplib

def send_email(subject, message, from_addr, to_addr):
    msg = 'Subject: {}\n\n{}'.format(subject, message)
    server = smtplib.SMTP('smtp.gmail.com', 587)
    server.ehlo()
    server.starttls()
    server.login(from_addr, 'your-password')
    server.sendmail(from_addr, to_addr, msg)
    server.quit()

send_email('Automation Update', 'The task was completed successfully.', 'me@example.com', 'you@example.com')
```

This Python script dispatches an email, through a Gmail SMTP server, with an update about task completion. Similarly, alerts can be set to flag issues encountered during automation tasks.

So, the question is not why to automate, but rather, why not? Automation, when done correctly, bestows upon our digital pursuits a sense of style and ease. It allows us to rise above routine tasks and emphasize strategic and creative tasks. Indeed, Excel automation, courtesy of Python, is probably the best gift technology has bequeathed to data analysts and professionals alike. It's not just about working hard anymore; it's about working smart. Python just helps you do that effortlessly.

Troubleshooting and Solutions

In the grand scheme of leveraging Python and Excel together, the introduction of automation might be nothing short of a blissful dream that has finally culminated into reality. However, like any dream that comes with challenges to overcome, automation and scripting with Python might expose us to a handful of issues. The beauty of it? Every problem comes with a solution, a mystery holding an answer in its crux. In this section, we'll take a tour of some common issues that might arise, along with practical solutions to resolve them, ultimately guiding you to an unimpeded journey in the world of Python and Excel.

Dealing with Import Errors

One of the most common issues, when using Python for automating tasks in Excel, relates to importing libraries. Here's how you can cater to them:

1. Ensure that the needed libraries have been installed.

2. Verify the library spelling is correct.

3. Confirm that the Python interpreter is the same as the one where the libraries are installed.

If you're facing issues with installing libraries, you might want to check your Python and pip versions and try running the installation with elevated privileges (using sudo on Mac/Linux).

Troubleshooting Excel File Not Found

Another classic issue is dealing with Excel files not found, especially when reading or writing to an Excel file using Python:

1. Validate if the file indeed exists at the specified path.

2. Check if the file path is correct. Remember, Python uses slashes ("/") and not backslashes for paths.

3. Make sure that the program has the necessary permissions to read/write the file.

Handling Automation Errors

Automation, although aimed at reducing human errors, might run into issues on its own.

1. For tasks failing to execute, check the logic inside your script, rerun the script, and monitor for any Python errors.

2. If the automation timing is incorrect, ensure the scheduling syntax is correct and verify your system's timezone settings.

3. For email alerts not sent, check the SMTP server settings and confirm that your program is successfully dispatching emails.

Debugging Python Scripts

Debugging scripts is an important part of troubleshooting. You can print variable values or use Python's inbuilt debugger (pdb) to resolve issues.

```python
import pdb
# Example code
def example_func(data):
```

```
# add pdb breakpoint
pdb.set_trace()
print(data)

example_func("Hello World")
` ` `
```

This code is a 'Hello, World!' example where a pdb set_trace() acts as a breakpoint. When Python executes the set_trace() it will pause execution, allowing you to inspect and change variables.

Handling Formatting Issues

Formatting issues can arise predominantly when reading or writing Excel files using Python.

1. Use the appropriate functions provided by Python libraries to set or modify Excel formats.

2. Check the datatypes of your data. Python could misinterpret Excel datatypes and you might need to manually specify them.

Remember, troubleshooting is not a detour, but an integral part of the programming journey. Each error is a lesson in disguise that only hardens your resolve and polishes your skills. So, when you encounter a hurdle, take it up as a challenge and try to resolve it by understanding what caused it. Python and Excel, when perfectly intertwined, can prove incredibly powerful, but the key to perfecting the blend is through navigating across potential roadblock, turning troubleshooting from an art to second nature. Keep pushing, keep decoding!

CHAPTER 6: IN-DEPTH PYTHON FOR EXCEL

Dealing with different types of data

Breaking into the melodious symphony of Python City and Excel County, we're introduced to the seasoned players: the data types. In an arena filled with activity, the need to recognize and distinguish between different types of data becomes imperative. A number is not just a number here, a date is more than a day on the calendar, and text, well, isn't only text. Python and Excel house characters of various kinds, making it a programmer's responsibility to dialog with all these types effortlessly. In this intriguing section, we will embark upon a voyage demystifying the different data types, their quirks, and how to master dealing with these types in Python and Excel.

In Python, numbers fall into three categories: Integers, floating point numbers, and complex numbers, each serving a unique purpose. Excel, on the other hand, treats numbers as 'General,' but provides a palette of formatting options like percentages, fractions or scientific notation. When Python interacts with Excel, the Python data types must complement with the Excel file specific data requirements.

Consider the below code for converting a Python float into a percentage in Excel:

```python
import openpyxl
wb = openpyxl.Workbook()

ws = wb.active
val = 0.45
ws['A1'] = val

percent = openpyxl.styles.numbers.FORMAT_PERCENTAGE
ws['A1'].number_format = percent

wb.save('percent_file.xlsx')
```

In this snippet, we're saving 0.45 (a float) in 'A1' in Excel and then changing its format to a percentage.

Text Categories: The Strings and their Floor

Strings in Excel are 'General,' but rich text features allow for parts of the strings to have varied formats. Python's string manipulation capabilties combined with Excel's rich formatting options provide a powerful platform for textual data handling.

Chronicle of the Date and Time

Dates and time are peculiar in Python and Excel. While Excel stores date and time as numbers, Python has the datetime library that allows detailed operations. Awareness of this difference is crucial for successful interaction between the two. Here's one way to write date into Excel:

```python
from datetime import datetime
import openpyxl

wb = openpyxl.Workbook()
ws = wb.active

ws['A1'] = datetime(2022, 8, 15)

wb.save('date_file.xlsx')
```

In this code, a date is created through Python's datetime object and then written to an Excel spreadsheet.

The Boolean Ballet

Booleans in Python have two dancers: 'True' and 'False' while Excel uses 'TRUE' and 'FALSE'. Python booleans, when written into Excel, are automatically capitalized.

```python
wb = openpyxl.Workbook()
ws = wb.active

ws['A1'] = True

wb.save('bool_file.xlsx')
```

This code, as elementary as it seems, writes a Python boolean into an Excel spreadsheet cell.

For data types not natively supported in Excel, like Python's complex number, ensure to convert them into a supported data type before writing them into Excel.

In this rich tavern of Python and Excel, dealing with different types of data is akin to conversing in different linguistic dialects. Not every dialect might be familiar, and some might be more difficult than the others, but the capability to appreciate and communicate effectively in these dialects is the hallmark of a proficient programmer. Flexibility is key, and each data type adds a different flavor to our programming language. And when these flavors blend harmoniously, captivating results can be produced, enriching our understanding of Python and Excel.

Integrating Python scripts in Excel

When the drumbeat of data analysis reverberates, stalwarts in their fields stand on either side of the spectrum. On one platform, we have Python, versatile and powerful, known for its prowess in data manipulation, analysis, and machine learning. On the other, is Excel, the long-celebrated champion of spreadsheets, famous for its easy, user-friendly interface and robust functionality. This section will explore how these two giants can join hands, thereby breaking barriers, opening new possibilities, and making data handling more efficient than ever. We will delve into the fascinating world of integrating Python scripts in Excel.

Bridging these two entities brings forth an opportunity to utilize the best of both worlds - Python's computational power coupled with Excel's intuitive interface. However, to accomplish this alchemical goal of technological fusion, we need our golden bridge - an Excel add-in called XLWings.

The Alchemy of XLWings

XLWings, a Python library, links Excel with Python in an intimate dance. Its strength lies in the ability to leverage Python scripts from the cozy confines of an Excel workbook and vice versa. Let's get a glimpse of the brilliant acrobatics that XLWings can perform:

```python
import xlwings as xw

# connect to your workbook
wb = xw.Book('example.xlsx')

# reference to a sheet
sht = wb.sheets['Sheet1']

# write a Python list to Excel
data = ['Python', 'Data', 'Analysis']
sht.range('A1').value = data
```

In this script, we first import XLWings. It connects to the 'example.xlsx' file. Next, we reference 'Sheet1'. Finally, the Python list 'data' is written to Excel in range 'A1'. Now, when you open your workbook, you'll see the data written in the cells. It's like weaving a tapestry of code between Python and Excel!

Elevating this beautiful integration, Python functions can

magically manifest themselves in Excel as User Defined Functions (UDFs). Imagine calling a Python function directly from an Excel cell! Let's examine a Python function that calculates the average of numbers, which we transform into an Excel UDF via XLWings:

```python
import xlwings as xw

@xw.func
def calculate_average(numbers):
    return sum(numbers) / len(numbers)
```

After writing this script to an Excel-readable Python file and setting up the function through the XLWings Excel add-in, we can use `=calculate_average()` in Excel as we would with a native Excel function.

The integration doesn't stop at static function calls. With Excel being the user interface, it's possible to automate tasks with a touch of interactivity. For example, a button in Excel can trigger a Python script. This opens up a realm of possibilities from automated report generation to real-time data analysis.

Python and Excel, when entwined, bring forth an elevated platform of versatility, interactivity, and efficiency, effectively transforming complex tasks into a cakewalk. As we navigate further into this symbiotic realm, our abilities to manipulate, analyze, and interpret data reach uncharted heights.

Exception Handling

In the world of data analysis, numbers are the bedrock upon which decisions are built, influencing the course of businesses and various other enterprises. It is imperative, therefore, that we manage these numbers with meticulous precision. As we marry Python and Excel, we unravel possibilities, both wonderful and complex. To dowse the complexity and keep the process running smooth, we introduce our ally - Exception Handling. This chapter signifies the importance of Exception Handling in bringing consistency and reliability when integrating Python scripts in Excel.

The concept of Exception Handling finds its roots in Python. As we tread deeper into the labyrinth of code, we might stumble upon unexpected or undesirable outcomes. These stumbling blocks, known as exceptions, encompass issues such as type errors, value errors, file not found errors, and others. If untreated, exceptions act as bottlenecks, stopping your code and breaking the flow of execution. However, just like an orchestra conductor handles a wrong note and keeps the melody flowing, Exception Handling in Python gracefully manages these mistakes, offering solutions whilst keeping the code running.

To get a better understanding, let's include exception handling in our Python code using `try` and `except` blocks:

```python
import xlwings as xw

try:
    wb = xw.Book('missing_file.xlsx')
except FileNotFoundError:
    print('The file does not exist, please check the file path.')
```

```
` ` `
```

With the `try` block, we attempt to run our code. If an exception is thrown, rather than breaking the code flow, we catch it in the `except` block and handle it gracefully. In this case, if the file 'missing_file.xlsx' does not exist, instead of an error stopping the execution, it will trigger a simple print statement informing us about the missing file. This provides us with a clear, user-set indication of the problem.

The Intersection of Python and Excel Exception Handling

In the hybrid world where Python scripts are infused into Excel, the responsibility doubles. There are two sets of Exceptions to be managed - Python's and Excel's. Python's Exception handling works efficiently in managing the Python induced exceptions. However, Excel has its own set of rules and possible exceptions. An element as simple as referencing to an invalid cell index can send the script spiraling into an error abyss:

```python
try:
    wb = xw.Book('example.xlsx')
    sht = wb.sheets['Sheet1']
    data = sht.range('A1048577').value
except IndexError:
    print('Cell index out of range. Excel allows only up to 1048576 rows.')
```

In the script above, if we reference a cell that falls outside of Excel's dimension limits, Python's Exception Handling jumps in to save the day. It catches the 'IndexError' providing a clear warning, which contributes towards solution-oriented debugging.

Efficient exception handling paves the way for robust and reliable scripts that can withstand the tests of wrong file names, cell range overflows, invalid datatypes and more. As we continue our exploration into the mysteries of integrating Python and Excel, Exception Handling stands as our guide, keeping us grounded and confident in the face of challenges. It assures us that even in a labyrinth of code, there are no cul-de-sacs, only new paths to be forged.

Advanced Automation Examples

As we embark on placing theory into practice, we venture into the realm of advanced automation examples. The union of Python and Excel has empowered us with tremendous capabilities, helping us to automate complex tasks with ease. Let's now dive deeper and explore a handful of advanced use-cases where Python manipulates Excel to achieve automation that is not just intelligent and efficient, but also dynamic in its response to a sea of data challenges.

A central aspect of financial analysis is forecasting, which involves predicting future numbers based on past data. Automating this process not only saves substantial time but also eliminates human-induced errors. By deploying Python scripts in Excel, we can easily automate the tedious process of financial forecasting:

```python
# Practical Example of Financial Forecasting
import pandas as pd
```

```python
import statsmodels.api as sm
import xlwings as xw

wb = xw.Book('data.xlsx')
sht = wb.sheets['Sheet1']

data = pd.DataFrame(sht.range('A2:B222').value)
data.columns = ['Date', 'Full Year Sales']

model = sm.tsa.statespace.SARIMAX(data['Full Year Sales'],
order=(1, 1, 1), seasonal_order=(1, 1, 1, 1))
results = model.fit()

forecast = results.get_forecast(steps=5)
sht.range('C2').value = 'Forecasted Sales'
sht.range('C3').options(index=False, header=False).value =
forecast.predicted_mean
```

This script automates forecasting for future sales through a Python library called `StatsModels`, using Seasonal Autoregressive Integrated Moving Average (SARIMA), a popular forecasting method. The resultant forecasted values can then be pushed back to Excel using Excel's xlwings library.

Automating Data Cleaning and Preprocessing

Dirty data is one of the most pressing problems analysts face. Incorrect or missing data can lead to biased or incorrect outputs. Using Python in conjunction with Excel, we can automate this data cleaning process:

```python
# Practical Example of Data Cleaning
import pandas as pd
import xlwings as xw

wb = xw.Book('dirty_data.xlsx')
sht = wb.sheets['Sheet1']

data = pd.DataFrame(sht.range('A1:F500').options(pd.DataFrame, index=False, header=True).value)

# Replacing NaN values with mean
data = data.fillna(data.mean())

sht2 = wb.sheets.add(name='Cleaned Data')
sht2.range('A1').options(index=True).value = data
```

In this script, we're taking a dataset from Excel that might have some missing values ('NaN'). We then use Python's pandas library to fill those empty cells with the mean value of the data inside each respective column. After cleaning, the data is transferred back into a new Excel sheet, automating the cleaning process reducing manual labour and time.

Efficient automation in Excel doesn't just enhance productivity; it's a journey towards optimized operations, opening doors to an advanced level of data handling. By combining the powers of Excel and Python, you set yourself on a course not only to excel in the data analysis field but also to revolutionize business operations, commanding intelligent solutions to diverse challenges. Eagerly embracing this journey, let's explore further into the endless opportunities Python brings to Excel.

Debugging Python Scripts

With the capacity to automate intricate tasks realized through the union of Python and Excel, let's venture into another pivotal concept; debugging Python scripts. This process is more than just an error detection mechanism, it serves as a compass guiding us through the labyrinth of complex code, leading us directly to the root of problems that impede our automation journey.

As we become more comfortable with Python and Excel, and our scripts grow in complexity, it's inevitable that we may encounter issues and errors in our code. Debugging becomes paramount not just for error solving, but also for understanding and optimizing your code.

An important aspect of debugging is understanding the types of errors you might encounter. In Python, there can be syntax errors, logical errors, and exceptions. Syntax errors are detected by the parser before the program runs, while logical errors result from incorrect algorithmic logic causing the program to behave unexpectedly. Exceptions, or runtime errors, occur during the execution of a program due to operations like division by zero or file operations on a non-existent file.

Python provides an exceptional tool for debugging called pdb, the Python debugger. It allows you to set breakpoints in your code, step through the execution of the script, examine the state of variables, and evaluate arbitrary Python code in the context of your program. Here's a brief example of how pdb can help debug an Excel data manipulation script:

```python
# Debugging an Excel Data Manipulation Script with pdb
import pandas as pd
import xlwings as xw
import pdb

wb = xw.Book('data.xlsx')
sht = wb.sheets['Sheet1']

data = pd.DataFrame(sht.range('A2:B222').value)
data.columns = ['Date', 'Sales']

pdb.set_trace()

# Here, we compare the sales figures to a threshold
data['Sales'] = data['Sales'].apply(lambda x: x if x > threshold else 0)
sht.range('C2').options(index=False,    header=False).value    = data['Sales']
```

In this script, we're reading data from an Excel file and performing an operation on the 'Sales' column. We used the `pdb.set_trace()` line to set a breakpoint at that line. When we run this script, execution pauses at our breakpoint - allowing us to slowly step through the following lines, inspect the values of our variables, and essentially 'peek under the hood' of our program.

Debugging comes with its own set of practices that you can

adopt for a smooth debugging experience, such as using clear variable names to avoid confusion; commenting code sections for easy readability; writing modular, reusable code; and regularly using print() statements to monitor variable values.

Embracing the art of debugging will accelerate your Python programming journey. When partnered with Excel, you gain the power to not only navigate complex pathways of automation, but also the ability to interrogate, understand, and optimize them. As we continue to explore the synergistic power of Python and Excel, let's carry with us the vital skill of debugging to unravel complexities, resolve issues, and unlock superior performance in our automation endeavors.

Introduction to Data Analysis with Python and Excel

Immersing ourselves deeper into the world of Python and Excel, our rich journey welcomes a new and powerful ally - Data Analysis. Harmonising the analytical power of Python, alongside the data manipulation ease of Excel, generates robust data analysis capabilities believed to be the realm of data scientists. This fusion not only empowers an individual with enhanced insights, but can also transform an entire organization's operational efficiency and strategic decision-making.

Pragmatically, in the field of business and finance, data is the lifeblood, pumping precious information through the veins of our organizations, powering decision-making, strategy development, and overall success. Capturing this data is one thing, understanding it is another, and that's where our duo of Python and Excel excels.

Python is renowned for its extensive machine learning libraries and powerful statistical operations. Coupled with Excel's data management and visualization features, they form an unbeatable allied force in the battleground of data analysis. This twofold mechanism empowers us to extract meaningful insights from raw, unprocessed data, unearthing critical trends, patterns, and correlations that otherwise could have been overlooked.

Consider a real-world scenario where a financial advisor needs to analyze a large dataset of mutual fund performance. The Excel spreadsheet contains thousands of rows with complex financial data that would be unwieldy and time-consuming to analyze manually. Employing Python's pandas library, the analyst can programmatically filter, sort, and process the data; implementing advanced statistical calculations with ease. Post analysis, the results can be integrated back into Excel; leveraging the software's potent graphing capabilities to visualize the patterns and trends, facilitating a comprehensive, easily digestible analysis report.

```python
# Pandas for Data Analysis
import pandas as pd

# Load Excel file
df = pd.read_excel('mutual_fund_dataset.xlsx')

# Analyze data using pandas
mean_return = df['Annual Return'].mean()
high_risk_funds = df[df['Risk'] == 'High']

# Integrate results back into Excel
```

```
high_risk_funds.to_excel('highrisk_mutual_funds.xlsx')
` ` `
```

Above we see a concise, yet powerful, illustration of how Python and Excel can perform symbiotically, demonstrating how effortlessly Python can analyze an Excel dataset, and then return the results back into an Excel file for further manipulation and presentation.

Data analysis with Python and Excel extends beyond just number crunching. With a sprinkle of creativity, you can add a narrative to your data, convey a story, and breathe life into static numerals. Remember, data on its own is valuable, but understanding what that data signifies, the story it tells; that's where the true value lies.

As we delve deeper into data analysis, let our journey equip us with strategies for harnessing this powerful combination, making data not just informative, but transformative. Prepare to explore descriptive statistics, visualization techniques, and advanced data analysis methods, as we continue to amplify Python and Excel's synergy power, making it an advantageous tool in your professional toolkit to drive powerful revelations from data.

Descriptive Statistics

Our expedition through the realm of Python and Excel now takes us into the fascinating world of descriptive statistics - painting a vivid portrait of data. With the power of Python, we can quickly generate valuable statistical insights, cast in Excel for intuitive understanding and ease of interpretation.

Descriptive statistics encapsulate central tendencies, measures of dispersion, and the distribution shape of a dataset. It provides a compact summary of a dataset, which can be a particular group of data points such as sales trends or customer demographics.

Python's statistical libraries, including NumPy and SciPy for mathematical operations, and pandas for data management, are fantastic tools for descriptive statistics. Pairing these with Excel's pivot tables, graphs, and histograms creates a streamlined data analysis process, making the comprehensive interpretation of data easier.

Consider a scenario where an investment analyst wishes to comprehend key statistical measures - mean, median, standard deviation, and variance of stock price performances. Python can expediently process this data, with the results smoothly integrated into Excel for easy visualization.

```python
# Import requisite Python libraries
import pandas as pd
import numpy as np

# Load data in Excel file
df = pd.read_excel('stock_prices.xlsx')

# Compute Descriptive Statistics
mean_price = np.mean(df['Price'])
median_price = np.median(df['Price'])
std_dev_price = np.std(df['Price'])
variance_price = np.var(df['Price'])
```

```
# Transfer results back to Excel file
data    =    [mean_price,    median_price,    std_dev_price,
variance_price]
result_df    =    pd.DataFrame(data,    columns=['Value'],
index=['Mean', 'Median', 'Std Dev', 'Variance'])
result_df.to_excel('output_descriptive_stats.xlsx')
` ` `
```

The example provides a snapshot of the potential power and simplicity at our disposal. The calculated measures, once fed back into Excel, can then be utilized to create engaging visuals such as charts and dashboards. Meanwhile, Excel's feature-rich platform allows users to deep-dive into individual data points through filters and slicers, thereby enabling an interactive data investigation and presentation that adds nuance to the descriptive statistics.

However, descriptive statistics aren't merely about number crunching. They breathe life into raw data that might otherwise remain abstract and unapproachable to most stakeholders. A project manager, for instance, could use descriptive statistics to quantify project timelines and progress, sharing stakeholders' understandable insights.

As we advance further into data analysis with Python and Excel, we continue to unravel the simplicity underlying sophisticated operations. Much like seasoned travellers navigating well-charted terrains, Python and Excel promise a comforting yet rejuvenating journey to all those willing to immerse themselves in the thrilling landscape of data analysis.

Above all else, remember that descriptive statistics serves as a lighthouse, illuminating your path through the oftentimes foggy realms of data so that you can chart your course with confidence. This powerful toolset, when wielded correctly, can transform data into stories, numbers into narratives, and the abstract into the concrete. It's an invaluable guide in our data-driven journey. Let's continue to discover how Python and Excel enhance this process in the following sections.

Data Visualization

Just as a painter uses brushes and palettes to bring landscapes to life, we as data analysts rely on the power of visualization to lend vibrancy to abstract numbers. Python and Excel, when used in tandem, can paint a captivating impressionist masterpiece of data that is as informative as it is intriguing. Our next destination on this expedition is the visually stunning territory of Data Visualization.

Data visualization is the representation of information in the form of tables, graphs, and charts, which makes data analysis and interpretation easier, more intuitive, and effective. Python, with its data visualization libraries like Matplotlib and Seaborn, enables us to create rich, detailed, and appealing plots and charts. These visualizations can further be transferred to Excel for embellishment with Excel's easy-to-use graphical capabilities.

Visuals created through Python can be customized extensively by changing the size, shape, color, and other characteristics of the plots. Let's consider a situation where a Data Analyst needs to visualize the sales trends and performances of different products. A bar chart could be an effective tool for this task.

```python
# Import Python Libraries
```

```
import pandas as pd
import numpy as np
import matplotlib.pyplot as plt

# Load data from an Excel file
df = pd.read_excel('sales_data.xlsx')

# Group the data by Product, calculate the total sales
grouped_sales = df.groupby('Product')['Sales'].sum()

# Create a Bar chart of the Sales
plt.bar(grouped_sales.index, grouped_sales.values)
plt.xlabel('Products')
plt.ylabel('Sales')
plt.title('Total Sales by Product')
plt.savefig('sales_plot.png')
plt.show()
```
```

This Python script reads the data, groups it by product, and calculates the sum of sales for each product. Finally, it creates a bar chart of the sales and saves it as an image file. The beauty lies in the simplicity of Python scripting, turning handful lines of code into a comprehensive data story.

We can import the saved image into Excel where it can be annotated or used alongside other data representations. The combination of Python's flexibility and Excel's user-friendly interface creates an unmatched synergy that allows for tailor-made, dynamic data storytelling. Excel's extensive data visualization tools, such as scatter plots, trend lines, and
```

conditional formatting, can further enhance the impact and comprehensibility of your data presentations.

Python's scripting freedom allows for creating layered, multi-dimensional visualizations effortlessly, while Excel provides a structure where diverse visualizations can coexist, intertwining to narrate a compelling data tale. The ability to visualize data effectively can make the difference between a average report and a spectacular one.

Our exploration of Data Visualization takes us into different landscapes within the realm of Python and Excel. The insights gained from this chapter are akin to experimental sketches, the individual strokes and shades of a painting that will contribute to the grand masterpiece we're creating: an indelibly informed approach to data analysis with Python and Excel. With every new concept we learn, we add another color to our palette, enabling us to paint a progressively richer, more nuanced picture of our data. In the next chapter, we delve into more complex brushes of our data painting - the Quantitative Data Analysis.

Quantitative Data Analysis

Divulging into the world of Quantitative Data Analysis is akin to plunging into a river of numbers where patterns, correlations, and outliers shape the current's flow. With Python's data analysis capabilities and Excel's robust feature set, we are equipped with the tools to navigate this river swiftly and efficiently. As countless data points collide and converge, every stream that we explore offers a unique perspective that helps illuminate the raw, undiluted story residing within our data.

Quantitative data analysis involves the systematic application of statistical techniques to the measurement of data. This type of analysis often deals with measurable quantities, such as quantities sold, percentages achieved, variables measured and numbers counted.

Python brings several robust libraries, such as Pandas for data manipulation and SciPy for scientific computation, into this analytical landscape. Let's consider an example of Python quantitatively analysing the sales data of a retail company to understand customer behaviour and product performance.

```python
# Import Library
import pandas as pd

# Load data from Excel
df = pd.read_excel('sales_data.xlsx')

# Calculate mean and standard deviation of Sales
mean_sales = df['Sales'].mean()
std_sales = df['Sales'].std()

# Find products with above-average sales
popular_products = df[df['Sales'] > mean_sales]

print('The mean sales is: ', mean_sales)
print('The standard deviation of sales is: ', std_sales)
print('Products with above-average sales are: ', popular_products['Product'].unique())
```

In this code snippet, Python calculates the mean and standard deviation for sales, valuable metrics used to understand the center and spread of the data respectively. Further, it identifies products with above-average sales, providing useful insights into customer preferences and product performance. Should the resulting data be extensive, Python possesses the prowess to even find patterns which might not be readily observable.

Where Python scripts sift through this semiotic deluge meticulously, Excel uses its powerful computational power and visual prowess to augment these insights and present them in digestible and decipherable ways. Whether you're creating pivot tables, conducting regression analysis, or using conditional formatting to uncover trends and patterns, Excel's user-friendly interface makes these processes straightforward.

An example of quantitative data analysis in Excel could involve using a lookup function to compare the performance of products across different regions. Formulas such as INDEX-MATCH or VLOOKUP, along with other advanced features, offer a methodical route to disentangle complex datasets, enabling a meticulous analysis of various components.

The journey of data analysis is akin to the act of zooming in and out of a shot with a camera, altering perspectives as per necessity. In Python's case, every analytical technique and method acts as various lenses with their unique capabilities and versatility. Contrastingly, Excel represents the camera's operations, with its various functionalities facilitating manipulation and concise display of the scene captured through Python's lenses.

As we complete this section, the intricate threads of Python and Excel weave together to illuminate the intertwined patterns within our quantitative analysis tapestry - a synergy that empowers us to unravel the mesmerising complexity of data. This intricate dance of data and analysis techniques elucidates the next steps in our data-driven symphony - Qualitative Data Analysis.

Qualitative Data Analysis

Just as we ventured into the number-driven landscapes of Quantitative Data Analysis, our exploration into data science continues further with the interestingly elusive terrain of Qualitative Data Analysis (QDA). Unlike its numerical counterpart, QDA is less about figures and more about comprehending complex phenomena by exploring data from a subjective perspective.

In the zoetrope of qualitative data, words, emotions, and experiences replace digits. This form of data analysis thrives on the less tangible aspects that fall between the cracks of quantifiable metrics: customer opinions, user feedback, survey responses, interview transcripts and more. We delve beyond the 'what' and 'how many' to explore 'why' and 'how'.

It is into this realm that Python, with its broad suite of Natural Language Processing libraries such as NLTK (Natural Language Toolkit) and TextBlob, emerges as a highly potent tool. These libraries allow us to conduct text analysis, sentiment analysis, topic modelling and so much more, thereby uncovering patterns and insights.

Consider this script below as an example, where we evaluate the sentiment of product reviews.

```python
```

```
# Import Library
from textblob import TextBlob

# Load Text Data from Excel
df = pd.read_excel('product_reviews.xlsx')

# Define function to calculate sentiment
def calculate_sentiment(review):
    return TextBlob(review).sentiment.polarity

# Apply function to reviews
df['Sentiment'] = df['Review'].apply(calculate_sentiment)

print(df.head())
```
` ` `

The script uses the TextBlob library to analyse the sentiment of product reviews in our dataset, appending a sentiment score to each review. This provides us a window into the customer mindset, helping us understand their perception of the product.

On the other side of the equation, Excel equips us with tools to process qualitative data in a way that retains the inherent richness and context of the data, whilst making it amenable to meaningful interpretation. Excel's text functions such as LEFT, RIGHT, MID or LEN, and features like Text to Columns are instrumental in cleaning and organising unstructured data.

Additionally, features such as conditional filtering, word clouds, and pivot tables add more depth to the analysis, allowing one to explore and visualize large volumes of textual data with ease. They facilitate the segregation of this data into manageable categories - a process of thematic content analysis that can be a goldmine of insights.

Python's libraries like matplotlib and seaborn can then be leveraged to offer interesting data visualisation of the analysed qualitative data. These visual aids, ranging from word clouds to sentiment distribution graphs, further support the interpretative process, often revealing formidable patterns and trends in subjective human experiences and opinions.

Understanding qualitative data is akin to listening in on the world's conversations and finding the narratives within. It's a fascinating journey that thrives on Python's analytical prowess and Excel's unruffled organization. As we dip our toes into this intricate dance of words and emotions, we inch closer to unravelling the mysteries of data and reveal its ability to narrate tales, both calculable and abstract.

CHAPTER 8: ADVANCED DATA ANALYSIS

Multivariate Analysis

Having navigated the winding paths of univariate and bivariate analysis, it is now time to venture into the captivating realm of multivariate analysis. Here, instead of limiting ourselves to examining one or two variables at a time, we go beyond to analyse the interactions between multiple variables simultaneously.

The crux of multivariate analysis lies in its ability to unravel the complex, intertwined relationships amongst several variables, often in ways which cannot be deciphered from singularly examining each variable. This analysis can unearth the influence of several factors on a certain characteristic or outcome, a chord that resonates strongly in diversified fields such as finance, marketing, health research, and more.

Multivariate analysis is an orchestra where Python plays a masterful conductor. Leveraging libraries such as Pandas for data manipulation, NumPy for numerical computations, and scikit-learn for machine learning, Python enables us to perform a range of multivariate techniques effortlessly. From Principal

Component Analysis (PCA), Multiple Regression, to Cluster Analysis and Factor Analysis, these elements of Python's arsenal serve as powerful weapons on the multivariate frontier.

Here's an example of a Python script performing PCA, a dimensionality reduction technique:

```python
# Import Libraries
from sklearn.decomposition import PCA
import pandas as pd

# Load Excel Data
df = pd.read_excel('multivariate_data.xlsx')

# Instantiate PCA with 2 Components
pca = PCA(n_components=2)

# Fit and Transform Data
transformed = pca.fit_transform(df)

# Create New DataFrame with Transformed Data
df_transformed = pd.DataFrame(transformed, columns=['PC1', 'PC2'])
```

This Python implementation of PCA reduces the dimension of data from multiple variables to a few Principal Components (PCs) which are linear combinations of the original variables. These PCs are constructed such that they capture the maximum amount of variation in the data set, allowing us to visualize and analyze high-dimensional data more comfortably.

However, it's crucial not to lose sight of how Excel stands shoulder-to-shoulder with Python in this stage of our data analysis voyage. Using Excel's native functionality or spreadsheet add-ins like XLSTAT, one can perform multivariate techniques such as discriminant analysis, factor analysis or canonical correlation right out of the familiar Excel interface.

Beyond these, Excel's Power Query and Power Pivot are potent tools that allow aggregating data from several sources and conducting data modelling. Excel's interactive pivot charts and slicers then offer a dynamic way to visualize and explore this multi-dimensional data.

While Python excels at automation and is unmatched in handling large datasets, Excel's simplicity and intuitiveness retain a firm position in the data analyst's toolkit. They are intertwined like two strands of a DNA, each a complement of the other. Together, they're an indestructible duo that transform the elusive realm of multivariate data into a playground of statistics, insights and decision making.

Delving into the realm of multivariate analysis thus marks yet another milestone in our odyssey, blending the sturdiness of Python's analytical heft and the finesse of Excel's interface capabilities. As we continue, the true multidimensional nature of data embeds itself deeper into our understanding, building a formidable foundation upon which our data analysis capabilities stand tall.

Hypothesis Testing

As we delve deeper into our analytical journey, a key cornerstone that stands before us emanates the importance of statistical reasoning - and the concept shining brightest at the nucleus of it is 'Hypothesis Testing'. When confronted with a plethora of variables and an ocean of data, formulating data-driven hypotheses and testing them is a powerful beacon to steer our analytical ship towards meaningful insights.

Hypothesis Testing provides a systematic methodology to make reasoned decisions about the populations we're studying based on sample data. In essence, a hypothesis is an educated presumption, a notion we assert to be true unless there's overwhelming evidence to the contrary. Hypothesis Testing provides the context to use sample data to either validate or nullify this hypothesis.

Python, with its treasure chest of statistical libraries like SciPy and StatsModels, extends a helping hand in this venture. For example, here's a simple Python script for testing a one-sample t-test using SciPy:

```python
# Import Libraries
from scipy import stats

# Load Excel Data
df = pd.read_excel('sample_data.xlsx')

# Perform One-Sample T-Test
t_statistic, p_value = stats.ttest_1samp(df['Variable'], popmean=100)
```

In this small script, we're testing the hypothesis if the mean of 'Variable' in our data is equivalent to 100. This is called a one-sample t-test, one of the simplest forms of hypothesis testing.

The 't_statistic' gives us the test statistic value while 'p_value' provides the probability of observing our data given the null hypothesis is true.

The concept of a 'p_value' introduces another key element of Hypothesis Testing - the Null Hypothesis (H0) and Alternative Hypothesis (H1). H0 is typically a statement of 'no effect' or 'no difference'. In contrast, the Alternative Hypothesis, H1, is what we want to establish, the potential claim we're testing. If the p-value is smaller than our chosen significance threshold (often 0.05), we reject the Null Hypothesis in favour of the Alternative Hypothesis.

Excel is not to be left behind in the journey of Hypothesis Testing. Built-in functions like "T.TEST" allow you to perform T-Tests directly, while the Data Analysis add-in extends your capabilities to performing z-tests and Chi-Square tests amongst others. Excel's visual capabilities further shine when representing the distribution of our variables or the critical region of our Hypothesis Tests.

Hypothesis Testing shines a light on the path to making data-driven decisions. It brings to the fore the significance of underlying statistical reasoning, ultimately underpinning the essence of advanced data analysis. When driven by the robust computational aptitude of Python and the accessibility and visualization prowess of Excel, Hypothesis Testing stands as a key pillar in our analytical journey. Going forward, this understanding will serve as an essential tool in our evolving analytical arsenal. The ability to articulate, test, and interpret hypotheses will ensure essential evidence-backed insights to guide our resolution-making.

Machine Learning Basics

Cracking open the lockbox of modern data-driven decision making, we unveil yet another dazzling component - Machine Learning. A suave subset of Artificial Intelligence, Machine Learning is that magic wand transforming how we interpret, understand, and leverage data for prediction, automation, and achieving an advantageous foothold in a data-abundant world.

Grounded in the practice of teaching machines to learn and make decisions from data, Machine Learning extrapolates patterns and insights from existing data to predict, analyze, and comprehend complex systems and phenomena. It's the wand that guides the prediction of customer behavior, the analysis of colossal datasets, and even the steering wheels of autonomous vehicles.

Python plays a pivotal role in wielding this contemporary marvel, boasting an ensemble of robust libraries tailor-made for Machine Learning. Libraries such as Scikit-Learn, TensorFlow and PyTorch have been the exemplary champions in this analytical spectacle. A basic Machine Learning program involves loading the data, preprocessing it, choosing a model, training it on the data, and finally evaluating its performance.

Here's a textbook example of a Python script implementing a simple linear regression model using Scikit-Learn:

```python
# Import Libraries
from sklearn.model_selection import train_test_split
from sklearn.linear_model import LinearRegression

# Load Excel Data
```

```
df = pd.read_excel('data.xlsx')

# Splitting Data
X = df.iloc[:, :-1].values
y = df.iloc[:, -1].values
X_train, X_test, y_train, y_test = train_test_split(X, y,
test_size=0.2, random_state=42)

# Initialize and Train Model
model = LinearRegression()
model.fit(X_train, y_train)

# Evaluate Model
accuracy = model.score(X_test, y_test)
` ` `
```

In this script, we're delineating a path from loading excel data to evaluating a simple linear regression model's accuracy. The Python ecosystem's beauty lies in the straightforwardness of such implementations, consequently promoting Machine Learning's acceptance among data practitioners.

Excel too holds its ground in the realm of Machine Learning. Although not as versatile as Python in the variety of models it can handle, Excel can support some fundamental Machine Learning operations. For example, the Solver and Analysis ToolPak in Excel make it possible to perform linear regression - a form of Machine Learning algorithm. As such, Excel remains an accessible platform for experimenting with Machine Learning principles.

The veritable charm of Machine Learning springs from the plume of its potentiality - from recognizing speech and handwriting, predicting stock prices, to crafting personalized recommendations. As we navigate deeper waters of the data world, the importance of Machine Learning only magnifies in bridging the gap between data inundation and meaningful data interpretation.

Mastering the rudiments of Machine Learning - the diverse array of algorithms, the methods to prevent overfitting, and understanding bias-variance tradeoff - these are all essential check-points of our progressive analytical expedition. It's a tool that has created a paradigm shift in data analysis, and at its helm, Python and Excel together find their place at the cutting edge of these techniques. When complemented with the basics of Data Analysis and Hypothesis Testing, Machine Learning opens newer frontiers in our journey of unearthing revealing insights from data.

Data Analysis Case Studies

Delving further into practicality, let's zoom in on real-world data analysis case studies that illustrate real-life applications of Python and Excel. These instances reflect how astute incorporation of these tools can result in potent solutions, reshaping strategies and driving decisions anchored in robust analytical reasoning.

Our first case hails from the realm of finance. A multinational banking corporation needed to analyse the credit risk profiles of its potential customers. Writing custom Python scripts, read data stored in Excel files, comprising abundant customer details. Armed with an arsenal of Python's predictive modelling libraries, the banking corporation could anticipate potential defaulters, enabling smarter, data-driven credit lending decisions. Furthermore, it generated insights in Excel through visualizations and pivot tables, facilitating accessible and interpretable reporting.

```python
# Python Script: Predictive Modelling for Credit Risk
import pandas as pd
from sklearn.model_selection import train_test_split
from sklearn.ensemble import RandomForestClassifier

# Loan Data
data = pd.read_excel('LoanData.xlsx')

# Feature and Target Variables
X, y = data.drop('default', axis=1), data['default']

# Train-Test Split
X_train, X_test, y_train, y_test = train_test_split(X, y, test_size=0.2, random_state=42)

# Random Forest Model
model = RandomForestClassifier()
model.fit(X_train, y_train)
y_pred = model.predict(X_test)

# Saving Predictions on Excel
predicted_df = pd.DataFrame({'Actual_Default': y_test, 'Predicted_Default': y_pred})
predicted_df.to_excel('Predicted_Defaults.xlsx', index=False)
```

This script demonstrates a simple predictive model using Python and Excel to handle credit risk analysis in the banking sector.

Another intriguing case emerges from the healthcare landscape. A leading hospital network capitalized on Python and Excel's might to optimize patient outcomes and enhance operational efficiency. By using Python scripts that accessed patient records stored in Excel, they identified patterns linking hospital-acquired infections to several factors like room type, length of stay, and previous hospitalizations. This valuable analysis drove policy changes, leading to a significant reduction in hospital-acquired infections. The results were conveniently shared with different departments using Excel's interactive dashboard features.

These case studies resonate with the colossal capabilities that Python and Excel, together, bring to the table. They shed light upon their far-reaching applications across a multitude of sectors, underlining their omnipresence. Whether it's risk analysis in finance or predictive analytics in healthcare, merging Python's programming prowess and Excel's intuitive interface delivers cutting-edge data solutions.

Remember – these studies are not the ceiling; they're the floor. On this analytical journey, we'll unearth more such practical illustrations that, hopefully, add perspectives, inspire unique solutions in your work, and open up newer vistas of applying Python and Excel in your data exploration endeavours. As we forge ahead, you'll appreciate this amalgamation's undeniable synergy, turning seemingly unintelligible data into a goldmine of actionable insights.

Advanced Analysis Tips and Tricks

For those who are enthusiastic to delve deeper into the power of Python and Excel, and to cultivate more advanced skills for complex data analysis, here comes a collection of essential tips and tricks. These ideas have been cherry-picked from experienced professionals who utilized Python and Excel together. Hence, even for an advanced user, there's always something new to learn and refine.

1. **Use Python for Heavy Data Processing**: When you're working with large datasets that make Excel sluggish, Python comes to the rescue. Libraries like Pandas and Numpy can handle huge data volumes and perform complex operations much faster than Excel. Once the dataset is more manageable, it can then be exported to Excel for further analysis and visualization.

```python
# Python Code: Using Pandas for big data
import pandas as pd

# Load big data
big_data = pd.read_csv('big_data_file.csv')

# Perform operations
big_data['new_column']    =    big_data['column1']    +
big_data['column2']

# Export to Excel
big_data.to_excel('new_data.xlsx')
```

2. **Excel PivotTables with Python**: PivotTables are a staple in Excel. However, you can create similar cross-tabulation tables using Python's Pandas as well. This is particularly handy when working with larger datasets that might slow down Excel.

```python
# Python Code: Creating Pivot Tables
import pandas as pd

# Load data
data = pd.read_excel('data_file.xlsx')

# Pivot table
 pivot_table = pd.pivot_table(data, values='sales',
index=['region'],
columns=['product'], aggfunc=sum)

# Write to Excel
 pivot_table.to_excel('pivot_table.xlsx')
```

3. **Automating Tasks**: One of Python's biggest strengths is automation. If you find yourself doing a repetitive task in Excel, it's a great candidate for Python automation. This could range from fetching online data and updating your spreadsheets to automating reports that need to be generated regularly.

4. **Apply User-Defined Functions in Excel**: Python allows you to write complex functions, not feasible in Excel. By using certain libraries, you can introduce Python functions in Excel.

This fosters a more sophisticated and nuanced environment for data manipulation and allows you to carve out personalized features to suit your needs succinctly.

5. **Useful Libraries**: Knowledge of Python libraries pertinent to Excel operations is a must. Libraries like openpyxl or xlwings allow reading, writing and manipulating Excel files, while seaborn or matplotlib aid in creating advanced plots. pyxlsb permits reading large Excel files faster, offering a substantial speed advantage.

Embracing this blend of Python's advanced data processing and Excel's superior report generating interfaces combine into a wholesome analysis power-pack. These tips and tricks are meant to enhance your data deciphering journey, making it more exciting and fruitful. Always remember – the trick is to balance the capabilities of both Python and Excel, leverage their strengths, and compensate for one's shortcomings with the other's prowess. Unravelling insights will become a more effortless, enjoyable, and enriching process as you advance, converting you from a mere data handler to a well-rounded data strategist.

Introduction to Data Cleaning

Unleashing the true potential of data analysis starts at the fundamental level - ensuring that the data being worked on is clean, precise, and ready to reveal insights. As you embark on this journey of mastering Python and Excel for advanced analysis, understanding and applying effective data cleaning techniques becomes imperative. Often considered an unglamorous part of data analysis, data cleaning in reality holds enormous significance.

Data, received in raw form from myriad sources, is often disorganized and ridden with discrepancies. These inconsistencies can range from missing values, outliers, incorrect formatting, typographical errors, or skewed data due to deliberate falsifications or measurement errors, amongst others. Each of these anomalies pose a stark threat to the integrity of your analysis. This is where the art and science of data cleaning and preparation comes into picture. It can be seen as a ritual that prepares data for a meaningful journey, from its raw, haphazard state to being the base of insightful decisions and forecasts.

```python
# Python Code: Detecting Missing Values
import pandas as pd

# Load data
data = pd.read_excel('data_file.xlsx')

# Detect missing values
na_values = data.isna()

# View DataFrame with Boolean values indicating missing data
print(na_values)
```

Excel and Python, combined, are excellent tools for facing this challenge. Excel, with its user-friendly interface enables easy spotting and rectification of errors. Python, on the other hand, offers useful libraries, such as Pandas and Numpy, that allow rigorous, efficient, and automated cleaning of large datasets.

Their prowess together forms a powerful force capable of taming even the wildest of datasets, transforming them into polished, valuable informational assets.

```python
# Python Code: Replacing Missing Values
import pandas as pd

# Load data
data = pd.read_excel('data_file.xlsx')

# Flexibly replace missing values
data.fillna(value=-9999,     method=None,     axis=None, inplace=True)

# View cleaned data
print(data)
```

It's essential to understand that data cleaning is not a one-size-fits-all approach. The strategies and techniques adopted depend heavily on the nature of the dataset, the intended analysis and the end goal to be achieved. A careful inspection to identify redundant, missing or incorrect data, devising appropriate strategies, and applying them meticulously constitutes the crux of the cleaning process.

While there's no definitive guide to how this can be achieved, understanding the context, exploring the data, and making judicious decisions play a pivotal role in effective cleaning. As you progress through this chapter, some common and broadly applicable techniques will be dissected and elucidated.

Alongside the technicalities, you will be led to space where you can value the nuances and subtleties of data cleaning and appreciate how it sets the stage for confident and comprehensive data analysis.

Remember, data cleaning may often seem a tiresome and thankless task. Yet, it's this rigor in the initial stage that guarantees the reliability of the insights drawn, and the success of the decisions made subsequently. As they say, well begun is half done.

Missing Data Treatment

Data, as it exists in the wild, often comes with gaps. Values sometimes go missing due to a myriad of reasons - from inadvertent omissions to deliberate withholding of information. Regardless of the cause, these lacunae provide us a challenge in our data analysis journey. This is about treating these absentees, or to be precise - the treatment of missing data.

So, why should missing data concern us? Incomplete data can lead to bias, make our analysis less robust and ultimately lead to invalid or inconsistent results. The matter is even more pressing when dealing with large datasets where thousands of data points might be missing.

Let's conceptualize a common scenario. Suppose a financial firm conducts a global customer survey, streaming live metrics to an Excel worksheet. Unsurprisingly, not all participants fill in every item, leading to a problem of missing data.

```python
# Python Code: Finding Missing Data
```

```
import pandas as pd

# Load survey data
survey_data = pd.read_excel('customer_survey.xlsx')

# Detect missing values
missing_values = survey_data.isnull().sum()

# Display the number of missing values in each column
print(missing_values)
```

The key to the treatment of missing data lies in understanding the pattern of the missing data, which broadly falls into three categories:

1. Missing Completely At Random (MCAR), where data missing is independent of any variable

2. Missing At Random (MAR), the missing data is related to some other variables but not with the missing data itself.

3. Not Missing At Random (NMAR), where data missing is related to the values of the missing data itself.

Each category requires a different treatment strategy - from simple techniques such as listwise or pairwise deletion to more complex ones like imputing with mean, median, or mode, regression imputation, or advanced machine learning methods such as K-Nearest Neighbors (KNN) and Expectation-Maximization (EM).

```python
```

```
# Python Code: Imputing with Mean
import pandas as pd

# Load survey data
survey_data = pd.read_excel('customer_survey.xlsx')

# Replace missing values with the mean
survey_data.fillna(survey_data.mean(), inplace=True)

# Display cleaned data
print(survey_data)
```

Each technique has its advantages and drawbacks. While deleting records may lead to loss of useful information, imputation can introduce bias. Hence, it's crucial to make an informed choice based on the nature of your data, the extent and the pattern of missingness, and what your subsequent data analysis hopes to achieve.

Data analysts should also keep in mind that some missing data might be better left as is. Especially in cases where the absence of data carries meaningful information.

The one enduring principle in treating missing data is to always be transparent about the techniques used. You're not just filling in the gaps; you're ensuring the robustness of your subsequent analyses, the accuracy of your insights, and the credibility of your work. For remember, in the realm of data analysis, an informed guess is always better than an ignorant certainty.

Outlier Treatment

In the realm of data, our unsuspecting protagonists aren't always the typical, well-behaved figures we expect them to be. Sometimes, we encounter mavericks that dare to stray from the flock, individuals we refer to as outliers. Outliers are values that diverge significantly from the bulk of the data. Just as a detective would not ignore an individual behaving anomalously in an investigation, neither should we brush aside these enigmatic outliers. This particular insight involves dealing with outliers in your data.

But why should those solitary figures capture our attention? Isn't the 'average' perspective sufficient? Outliers can be immensely insightful, revealing previously unseen patterns, errors, or anomalies. They might indicate variability in your data, experimental error, or a novelty. However, they can also obscure the real trends and skew the statistical parameters. We don't wish to be guided by the whims of these outliers, no matter how intriguing they might be. Thus, we must 'treat' them.

Take a scenario where you're analyzing financial data, using Python to read this data from an Excel worksheet. Outliers could skew the results, making your analysis less accurate.

```python
# Python Code: Detecting Outliers using Z-score
import pandas as pd
from scipy.stats import zscore

# Load financial data
financial_data = pd.read_excel('financial_data.xlsx')

# Calculate Z-scores
```

```python
z_scores = zscore(financial_data)

# Find outliers
outliers = financial_data[(z_scores < -3) | (z_scores > 3)]

# Display the outliers
print(outliers)
```

The Z-score method, as shown above, is a common approach for outlier detection using standard deviation. Nonetheless, the outlier treatment strategy will depend on what caused the outlier, the extent of the outlier, its impact, and the specific requirements of your analyses.

There are several ways to treat your outliers:

1. **Exclusion**: The easiest method is to exclude the outliers. However, this approach can lead to loss of information.

2. **Imputation**: Replace the outlier with appropriate values.

3. **Transformation**: Transform the data to bring the outliers closer to the average.

4. **Binning**: Group the data into bins to smooth out the impact of outliers.

```python
# Python Code: Handling Outliers by Binning

# Convert Age to string type
```

```
financial_data['Age_Bins']    =    pd.cut(financial_data['Age'],
bins=[0,20,50,80,100], labels=['Young', 'Adult', 'Senior', 'Old'])
```
` ` `

In the above Python code, the 'Age' outliers are binned into categories like Young, Adult, Senior, and Old, thereby dealing with outliers by grouping them.

The notable truth is, outliers are unique - they need to be studied and treated on a case-by-case basis. Just like the missing data, the power to handle outliers wisely comes with the understanding of your data. The challenge is to strike that perfect balance where outliers don't significantly skew our analyses but continue to give us a broader perspective.

Proper outlier treatment allows for more dependable statistical parameters, enriched visualizations and more accurate models. It unearths the story of the data minus the disproportionate influence of an ostentatious few. The show must go on, and it is our job to ensure the spotlight shines where it truly matters. And so, with outliers aptly managed, we're a step closer to our climax of analysis.

Data Transformation

In a theatrical play, the actors may need to change costumes, or sets might need to be shifted around to narrate the story effectively. Similarly, data transformation is akin to changing the costume of raw data to align it with the plot of our analysis better. Data transformation is the procedure of converting data from one form or structure into another. The objective behind altering the state of data is to prepare it for ensuing stages of analysis.

Let's imagine ourselves in a scenario where we are analyzing annual revenues of firms listed in an Excel spreadsheet. Python is our tool of choice to examine this data. We intend to apply some form of time-series analysis. However, our dataset has revenues reported in multiple currencies. Herein lies the need for data transformation – to convert all the revenues into one standard currency, say, US Dollars. But how do we do it?

```python
# Python Code: Currency Conversion
import pandas as pd

# Load the dataset
financial_data = pd.read_excel('financial_data.xlsx')

# Conversion rates
exchange_rates = {'GBP': 1.36, 'EUR': 1.18, 'JPY':0.0093}

# Convert to USD
for i, row in financial_data.iterrows():
  currency = row['Currency']
  revenue = row['Revenue']
  financial_data.at[i,    'Revenue']    =    revenue    *
exchange_rates[currency]
```

In the Python code above, we create a dictionary `exchange_rates` that holds currency conversion rates from other currencies to USD. Subsequently, we iterate through our `financial_data` DataFrame, converting the 'Revenue' entries to USD based on their current currency.

Data transformation is not a one-size-fits-all approach. It is a broad category comprising various methods. Let's zoom into a handful:

1. **Normalization**: It is a scaling technique where values are shifted and rescaled so that they end up ranging between 0 and 1.

2. **Standardization (Z-score normalization)**: This method transforms the data to have zero mean and standard deviation of 1, thereby aligning with a standard normal distribution.

3. **Log Transformation**: This is particularly useful when dealing with skewed data. It can help to pull in long tails.

4. **Binning**: Binning is the process of transforming numerical variables into categorical counterparts. An example of this was demonstrated in the outlier treatment section.

5. **Dummy Variables**: Used for coding categorical variables into a series of binary (0 or 1) variables.

```python
# Python Code: Data Transformation using z-score
standardization
from scipy.stats import zscore

# Compute z-scores
financial_data['Revenue_zscore']                    =
zscore(financial_data['Revenue'])
```

In the Python code above, we use the `zscore()` function from `scipy.stats` to standardize the 'Revenue' column.

Data transformation is your secret toolkit when modifying and polishing your data, readying it for the limelight. Consistent with the play analogy, appropriately 'costumed' versatile data ready for any analysis scene is a dream for any director. In this case, you, the Python conductor, set the stage for the curtain raiser - getting ready for the grand finale of machine learning or advanced statistical analyses.

In the next section, your role changes to that of a meticulous painter, ready to turn the data canvas into a preparatory masterstroke for analysis. So, let us march forward and get those brushes ready!

Preparing Data for Analysis

Stepping into the shoes of a strategic general, readying your troops for the crucial battle that lies ahead, data preparation for analysis is a stage where the true potential of Python and Excel come to light. You map out the terrain, understand the strengths of your arsenal, devise strategies to deal with the unknown, and ultimately set up your ranks for the pinnacle of data science - the analysis.

Let's traverse this terrain carefully. Data prepared for analysis becomes a powerful chess piece that could checkmate the most complex analytical queries. However, this phase is often characterized by various roadblocks ranging from missing entries to repetitive data. So how does one employ Python and Excel strategically to conquer this stage?

Consider Excel as your tried and trusted lieutenant, sketching the initial battle plans. Fundamental spreadsheet manipulations like adding calculated fields, filtering data using 'Sort & Filter' tool and transforming data to its appropriate 'number form' could be handled at this level. Python, the decorated general riding a chariot of assorted libraries, advances this initial plan into actionable strategies.

```python
# Python Code: Data Preparation using scikit-learn library
from sklearn.model_selection import train_test_split

# Splitting data into training and test sets
train_data, test_data = train_test_split(financial_data, test_size=0.3, random_state=42)
```

Here we use scikit-learn's `train_test_split()`, a function that randomly bifurcates our dataset into a training set and a test set.

Broadly, elements on our checklist to effectively prepare data for analysis include:

1. **Handling null or missing values**: From outright deletion to advanced imputation techniques, our strategies to plug gaps in our data are crucial.

2. **Dimensionality Reduction**: Too many variables or features may confuse our analytical models. Techniques like Principle Component Analysis (PCA) ensure we fight this wisely.

3. **Feature Engineering**: Creating new variables that encapsulate relevant information in one can provide a bird's eye

view of the field.

4. **Data Partitioning**: Often, we divide data into distinct sets (Train, Validate, and Test), each fulfilling different roles in the battle.

5. **Balancing Data**: Ensuring each category or class in your data is proportionately represented avoids biases in battle outcomes.

What follows is an example illustration.

```python
# Python Code: Dimensionality Reduction: PCA example
from sklearn.decomposition import PCA

# Apply PCA
pca = PCA(n_components = 2)
financial_data_pca = pca.fit_transform(financial_data)
```

In this code, we are using the PCA method from Python's scikit-learn library. It reduces the dimensionality of our financial data to two principle components.

Strategically enlisting Python and Excel's capabilities in preparing data effectively sets up our analytical battle map. Latent trends are exposed, hidden patterns unveiled, and meaningful relationships between variables rise like phoenixes from the data dust.

Embrace the strategic general within you, for we are advancing to the front lines of the battle in the forthcoming sections.

The war drums of machine learning algorithms and advanced analytical techniques echo in the horizon, so let's march on, prepared and unwavering!

CHAPTER 10:
AUTOMATING EXCEL
TASKS WITH PYTHON

Fundamentals of Automation

In the bustling metropolis of today's business world, where digital timestamps swiftly cover digital footprints, one cannot disregard the power that automation wields. As data analysts, we play the part of the city's grand engineer, leveraging the tools of Python and Excel to architect an intricate neural grid of automation systems, ensuring smooth, seamless, and efficient operation. The heart of this grid is our understanding and application of automation fundamentals.

Python and Excel, two highly potent tools when used in conjunction, present us with a generous palette of automation capabilities. But before we paint our canvas, let us understand our colours - the basics of automation.

In the simplest of terms, automation is replacing manual tasks with systems or processes that can function without human intervention. It's like substituting manual gatekeepers with an automatic gate that opens when it detects an approaching vehicle.

From an Excel perspective, even our spreadsheet forerunners have, at times, dabbled with automation. They harnessed Excel's inbuilt tools such as Formulas, PivotTables, Macros, VBA scripts to run complex calculations, generate reports or organise data, without needing to manually operate each step.

Let us take a quick look at an Excel VBA code example that automates the creation of a new sheet:

```Excel VBA
Sub AddNewSheet()

    Sheets.Add(After:=Sheets("Sheet1")).Name = "NewSheet"

End Sub
```

Here, the Excel VBA script creates a new worksheet after a worksheet named "Sheet1" and renames the new worksheet to "NewSheet," thereby eliminating the need for us to perform these steps manually.

Python, our grand maestro of automation, takes this a step further. Python, with its armada of powerful libraries like pandas, numpy, openpyxl and many more, can turn routine tasks such as data extraction, analysis, visualisation and report generation into ongoing processes. Python scripts can shuffle vast data decks into neat piles or commands that can extract meaning from an ocean of data with a single line of code.

Consider the following Python script:

```python
# Python Code: Automating Data Analysis with Pandas
import pandas as pd

# Loading the data
data = pd.read_csv("financial_data.csv")

# Automate descriptive statistics generation
descriptive_statistics = data.describe()

```

Here, we read a CSV file using Python's pandas library and automatically generate descriptive statistics with the `describe()` function. Once properly set up, we can run this script anytime, and it would crunch the numbers for us without any manual intervention, regardless of whether our dataset is a mere pond of numbers or a vast sea of digits.

At its heart, the essence of the fundamentals of automation lies in the transferral of human effort onto intelligent systems. It's about creating a sophisticated dance between Python and Excel, letting them waltz through colossal amounts of data, finding patterns and spewing insights as they twist and turn through rows and columns.

Practical Examples of Automated Tasks

As the music swells, Python takes center stage, flourishing its capabilities, ready to demonstrate how it can synchronize with Excel to choreograph an impressive spectacle of automation. In this section, we venture into the realm of practicality, where theory meets application, as we explore real-world examples of automated tasks using Python and Excel. These tasks, once tedious, manual, and mundane, now evolve into an efficient, precise, and prompt process, thanks to Python's automation capabilities.

Before we pull back the reins and propel ourselves, let's understand this - the real leap with Python isn't about eliminating the need for Excel; it's about expanding Excel's horizons by automating tasks that would have been extremely time-consuming, expensive, or even impossible within Excel alone.

Let's quickly dive into some tangible examples:

1. Data Cleaning and Preparation:

Data rarely arrives in a ready-to-analyze state. Python's vast collection of powerful libraries, such as pandas and NumPy, quickens the scrubbing and scouring of data, ensuring it's clean, organized, and ready for analysis. Here's a small pandas magic trick that imputes missing values:

```python
# Python code to handle missing data

import pandas as pd

# Loading the data
data = pd.read_csv("dirty_data.csv")

# Fill missing values with the mean of the column
```

```
data = data.fillna(data.mean())
```

In this example, Python efficiently selects and fills-in missing data in our dataset, utilizing the mean value. Imagine performing this task manually in a vast dataset using Excel!

2. Merge and Combine Data:

Python shines when you need to merge datasets from different sources or combine various Excel files. Below is a Python code snippet that coolly combines several Excel files into a single one:

```python
# Python code to merge excel files

import pandas as pd
import os

all_files = [file for file in os.listdir() if file.endswith('.xlsx')]

data_combined = pd.concat([pd.read_excel(file) for file in all_files])

data_combined.to_excel("Combined_file.xlsx", index=False)
```

Here, Python subtly automates the formerly laborous task of opening numerous excel files and combining data. A task savored only by the truly masochistic ones amongst us.

3. Refresh Excel Charts:

Fancy a refreshment? Excel charts sure do. Python pushes the automation lever up again by refreshing Excel charts every time the underlying data changes. Check out this example using the openpyxl Python library:

```python
# Python Code to refresh excel charts

from openpyxl import load_workbook

# load excel file
wb = load_workbook('finance_data.xlsx')
ws = wb.active

chart = ws.charts[0]
chart.refresh()

```

Here you see, Python ensures the Excel chart automatically gets updated whenever there's a change in the underlying data. A small step for Python, a giant leap for data analysis!

As we traverse further, unmasking Python's automation prowess, such examples will increasingly become your everyday magic tricks, your new normals, as you dance with Excel and Python, waltz with data, and spin beautiful insights.

Scheduling Automated Tasks

The crescendo in our symphony of automation hits its

peak when Python, once more, conducts a masterstroke by shouldering the responsibility of scheduling automated tasks. Python's ability to schedule tasks can be a godsend, especially when dealing with tasks that need to function without continuous human intervention, such as maintaining updated data reports or sending out regular automated emails.

Let us weave in the magic of automation that has Python at its helm. We will be using Python's 'schedule' library, a simple, in-python library designed to execute jobs at given intervals.

1. Automating Data Updates:

Imagine you are running a financial report that feeds from various data sources. It's crucial to keep this report updated. Let's see how Python can automate this for us:

```python
# Python Code to Automate Data Updates

import schedule
import time

def task():
    print("Database updating...")
    # code to perform data updating goes here.

schedule.every(10).minutes.do(task)

while True:
    schedule.run_pending()
```

```
    time.sleep(1)
` ` `
```

In this cunning piece of code, Python automates database updating every 10 minutes using the 'schedule' library, giving you up-to-the-minute financial insights. This allows you to focus on analysing the data, rather than consistently worrying about its recency.

2. Scheduling Automated Emails:

Another common usage of automation in workplaces is scheduling emails, particularly ones that are repetitive and need to be sent at regular intervals. Let's see Python taking up the baton for us:

```python
# Python Code to Schedule Email

import schedule
import time
import smtplib
from email.message import EmailMessage

def send_email():
    server = smtplib.SMTP('smtp.gmail.com', 587)
    server.starttls()
    server.login("Your email here", "password")

    msg = EmailMessage()
    msg.set_content("Email body")
```

```python
msg['Subject'] = "Subject"
msg['From'] = "Your email"
msg['To'] = "Recipient email"

server.send_message(msg)
server.quit()

schedule.every().day.at("10:00").do(send_email)

while True:
    schedule.run_pending()
    time.sleep(60) # wait one minute
```

In this script, Python sends out an automated email every day at 10 AM. Just imagine the amount of time saved on sending routine emails!

3. Performing Regular Data Backups:

Data is the lifeblood of any financial operations and thus must be backed up regularly. With Python, data backup can be carried out seamlessly and automatically.

```python
# Python Code to Perform Data Backup

import schedule
import time
import os
import shutil
```

```python
def backup():
    source_folder = "/path/to/source_folder"
    backup_folder = "/path/to/backup_folder"
    shutil.copytree(source_folder, backup_folder)

schedule.every().friday.at("23:45").do(backup)

while True:
    schedule.run_pending()
    time.sleep(60)  # wait one minute
```

```
```

Here, Python elegantly performs data backup every Friday at 23:45, ensuring that your critical data is always secure, and without the need of a reminder.

This operation is analogous to setting a long-play record and allowing the resonant notes of Python's automation capabilities to wind through your daily tasks. As you delve deeper into this symphony, it becomes apparent that automation with Python is not a mere dalliance, but the real game changer in driving efficiency in an Excel-centric environment.

Troubleshooting Automated Tasks

While the symphony of Python's automation capabilities can reverberate through Excel activities with great ease, one might occasionally encounter a few discordant notes. Despite the apparent simplicity of automating tasks, some possible roadblocks can put a spoke in our automation wheel. Fear not, brave scriptwarriors, for this section is about cutting through these knots and tangles, conquering any hurdles, and restoring harmony to your automated tasks.Many issues related to scheduling and execution of automated tasks can be traced back to faulty scripts, unhandled exceptions, and environmental inconsistencies.

1. Compliance with Task Schedules:

One common glitch that could occur is the mishap of automation tasks ignoring the schedules set for them. Python's 'schedule' library relies on real-time, small delays could pile up over time, causing significant deviations. In such cases, consider using a more robust scheduling solution like cron on Unix-based systems, or Task Scheduler on Windows, which can guarantee execution at the exact time.

2. Unhandled Exceptions:

Any unhandled exception in an automated task will halt the process and disrupt the automation flow. Although Python boasts robust error-handling capabilities, it requires diligent programming effort to capture and handle all possible exceptions. Errors such as file-not-found, database connection failures, or network issues need to be anticipated and mitigated with a well-placed try/except block:

```python
# Python Code to Handle Exceptions

import schedule
import time

try:
```

```
def task():
    print("Database updating...")
    # Code to perform data updating goes here

schedule.every(10).minutes.do(task)

while True:
    schedule.run_pending()
    time.sleep(1)

except Exception as e:
    print(f"Caught following exception: {e}.")

` ` `
```

This example cleverly illustrates how Python can catch and display unexpected errors, helping you to understand what went astray.

3. Environmental Inconsistencies:

Your scripts might run flawlessly in one environment and fail in another. Eventual differences in operating systems, Python versions, library versions, or system configurations can cause unexpected issues. Maintaining consistency across operating environments can save you from hours of troubleshooting. Using virtual environments like 'venv' in Python can isolate your application and provide its required dependencies.

4. Test Thoroughly Before Automating:

Automation is designed to save time, but improper

implementation can result in the opposite. Before you automate any process, ensure that the task runs flawlessly in manual mode multiple times. This can help in detecting hidden snags that cause errors when automated.

5. Logging and Exception Notification:

Automated tasks often run in the background and a well-designed logging mechanism is a must-have to keep tabs on their proceedings. All significant events, exceptions, or errors should be logged. Moreover, serious exceptions should be communicated to the appropriate personnel via an exception notification system like sending an automated email:

```python
# Python Code to Send Automated Email upon Exception
import smtplib
import traceback

try:
    # Code to perform data updating goes here

except Exception as e:
    error = traceback.format_exc()
    server = smtplib.SMTP('smtp.gmail.com', 587)
    server.starttls()
    server.login("Your email here", "password")
    subject = "An Exception Occurred in Your Python Script"
    body = f"The following error occurred in the script: \n{error}"
    message = f'Subject: {subject}\n\n{body}'
```

```
server.sendmail(
  "From email",
  "To email",
  message)
server.quit()
```
```

In a utopian world of seamless automation, troubleshooting would be a scarce necessity. However, in reality, troubleshooting is a crucial partner in the dance of automation. With the insights from this section, you're equipped to unmask these errors, fix them, and orchestrate a flawless performance of your automated tasks.

## Excel and Python Automation Best Practices

In the versatile theatre of Python and Excel, automating tasks is akin to a well-choreographed ballet. Each component gracefully moves in sync, delivering eons of work in mere seconds. However, this all-star performance blossoms when directed according to best practices. As we journey down this final chapter's labyrinth, let's take a moment to extract wisdom from veterans, focusing on automation best practices that fuse the power of Python and Excel into one captivating spectacle.

**1. Modularize Your Code:**

Devise your automation scripts into modular units with each function fulfilling one precise task. This practice eases troubleshooting, enhances readability, and encourages code reuse.
```

```python
# Modular Python Code
def read_data(file_path):
    # Code to read data from file

def process_data(data):
    # Code to process data

def write_data(data, file_path):
    # Code to write data to file

def automate_task():
    data = read_data('input.xlsx')
    processed_data = process_data(data)
    write_data(processed_data, 'output.xlsx')

automate_task()
```

In this sample, each function performs a distinct task - reading, processing, and writing data. The main function, `automate_task()`, encapsulates the entire process.

2. Use Version Control:

Keeping track of modifications to automation scripts over time is imperative. A version control system like Git allows you to navigate this forest with sure footsteps, ensuring data integrity and collaboration efficacy.

3. Employ Error Handling and Logging:

We've flirted with error handling and logging extensively in the previous section. Exploiting it preemptively and judiciously is a particular watchword within best practices.

4. Consider Scalability and Maintainability:

A wise developer always crafts code with future challenges in mind. As your automation needs twist and swell, so should your scripts. Ensuring they're easily scalable and maintainable is a tenet of automation best practices. The key here is simplicity - complex problems are best solved with simple solutions.

5. Automate Incrementally:

Automation is not a volcano that erupts all at once. Do not rush to automate everything in one swoop. Instead, like a thoughtful baker, knead your automation dough slowly, methodically, one piece at a time.

6. Document Your Code:

In the winding lanes of code, comments are your street signs. They guide future travelers (or your future self) swiftly. Every complex functionality should be accompanied by clear, concise comments explaining its raison d'être.

```python
# Correct way to comment code
def process_data(data):
```

```
"""

This function processes the data by performing X, Y, and Z

Args:
data: a Dataframe containing the data to be processed

Returns:
processed_data: a Dataframe containing the processed data
"""

# Code to process data
```

7. Voluntary Code Reviews:

A fresh pair of eyes can spot what tired eyes may miss. Regular code reviews can neutralize latent bugs, enforce coding standards, and breed knowledge sharing.

CHAPTER 11: REAL-WORLD PROJECTS

Custom Financial Dashboard

In the architectural treasury of Python and Excel that we have explored together thus far, building a bespoke financial dashboard is akin to sculpting a masterful fresco. This could represent data, parsed and processed through Python, incorporated into the accessibility, flexibility, and interactivity that Excel provides. Now, with our well-tailored financial cloak adorned, let's delve into building a custom financial dashboard - a guardian against bewildering financial data that gives us a glance-view of related metrics.

Financial dashboards, often the canary in a financial coal mine, provide real-time visual feedback regarding financial performance. The amalgamation of Python and Excel presents us with an enticing possibility - a dashboard that's not just a report but a real-time, interactive, and dynamic companion on our financial expedition.

Let's imagine a scenario of consolidating Income Statements from multiple business units in your company. Each unit markets its Income Statement as an Excel file daily. We have to create a dashboard that provides real-time insights on key performance indicators (KPIs) like Revenue, Costs, and ultimately, Net Income.

How do we tackle this challenge?

First, our Python script needs to pull data from those Excel files. The `pandas.read_excel()` function allows Python to beckon Excel data seamlessly.

```python
import pandas as pd

# Read the data
df1 = pd.read_excel('Income Statement BU1.xlsx')
df2 = pd.read_excel('Income Statement BU2.xlsx')
```

Next, armed with pandas' data manipulation power, we clean, transform, and amalgamate these datasets into a form suitable for our dashboard.

```python
# Concatenate datasets
data = pd.concat([df1, df2], axis=0)

# Calculate the KPIs
revenue = data['Revenue'].sum()
costs = data['Operating Costs'].sum()
net_income = revenue - costs
```

With our KPIs meticulously computed, it's time to push these back to our Excel dashboard.

```python
# Write the KPIs to our dashboard
dashboard = pd.read_excel('Dashboard.xlsx')
dashboard.loc[0, 'Revenue'] = revenue
dashboard.loc[0, 'Costs'] = costs
dashboard.loc[0, 'Net Income'] = net_income
dashboard.to_excel('Dashboard.xlsx', index=False)
```

We can extend this script to include additional functionalities such as sending automated mail notifications when income or expense cross certain thresholds, triggering actions, and showcasing trends. This Python-Excel duo also allows us to enrich the dashboard further with colourful charts, graphs, pivot tables, conditional formatting, dropdown filters, and dynamic controls like sliders and radio buttons!

Remember, this is just an illustrative guide to constructing a custom financial dashboard, and the real-world applications can be even more profound and complex. Now, bask in the glory of your custom dashboard, ever vigilant, proactive, and dynamic, much like you on your finance adventure. Remember the underlying principles - clean your data, calculate your KPIs, and push back the insights in an easily consumable form. Happy dashboarding!

Automated Report Generation

Automated report generation is like a skillful orchestra conductor, harmonizing the discordant scores of data into a symphony of insightful business intelligence. As financial professionals, we deal with voluminous data and pressing timelines. Our Python-Excel ensemble, faithful allies, steps up to the stage here. Are you ready? Let's embark on a quest to automate report generation, transmuting raw data into action-driving intel under Python's guiding baton and Excel's splendid performance.

Consider the case where you are tasked with generating monthly financial performance reports from raw transactional data. Time-consuming if done manually for each department, but that's where Python wields its magic.

Let's begin by gathering our raw data into Python's realm using `pandas.read_excel()`:

```python
import pandas as pd

# Reading the data
raw_data = pd.read_excel('RawTransactions.xlsx')
```

The raw data, once in our grasp, needs tidying and transforming. We filter data for each department, summarize it on key parameters like income, expenses, and profit margin, and repeat this for each department:

```python
# Filtering the data for a department
data_dept_A = raw_data[raw_data["Department"] == 'A']
```

Summarizing the data

```python
summary_A = data_dept_A.groupby('Month').agg({'Income': ['sum'], 'Expenses': ['sum']})

summary_A['Profit Margin'] = (summary_A['Income'] - summary_A['Expenses']) / summary_A['Income']
```

With departmental summaries at hand, it's time to transport this informative payload back into Excel using `pandas.DataFrame.to_excel()`. Python scribes these reports into separate worksheets, tailoring each to departmental fingerprints:

```python
with pd.ExcelWriter('MonthlyReport.xlsx') as writer:
    summary_A.to_excel(writer, sheet_name='Dept_A')
```

As in a complex symphony, this can't be it! Usher in Excel to add vivid formatting, charts, and pivot tables, making our pandas-powered number crunching more tangible and comprehensible. We can do this by levying Excel libraries like `openpyxl` or `XlsxWriter`, which give us scripting access to Excel's eye-catching aesthetics:

```python
import openpyxl as oxl
from openpyxl.chart import BarChart, Reference
```

Load workbook

```
book = oxl.load_workbook('MonthlyReport.xlsx')
writer.sheets = dict((ws.title, ws) for ws in book.worksheets)

# Add a bar chart for department A
sheet = book['Dept_A']
chart_A = BarChart()
values = Reference(sheet, min_col=2, min_row=1, max_col=4, max_row=12)
chart_A.add_data(values, titles_from_data=True)
sheet.add_chart(chart_A, "E5")

# Save it
book.save('MonthlyReport.xlsx')
` ` `
```

Our symphony concludes on a high note, having transformed scattered raw data notes into a beautiful composition of insightful departmental reports. Reports are no longer a manual task, but an automatic one, saving time, increasing accuracy, and providing actionable financial insights. Embrace this automated bliss, for in the next act, we plunge into the realm of web data scraping and analysis.

Data Scraping and Analysis

Data scraping and analysis is the digital-age treasure hunt, where Python serves as our trusty map for navigating through the vast oceans of the internet, and Excel is our adept treasure chest for storing and organizing our precious findings. It's a powerful collaboration, a dynamic duet composed of Python's web scraping abilities and Excel's data analysis prowess that help us extract actionable intelligence from the boundless resource that is the world wide web.

Let's say you are a financial analyst needing to track certain stocks' performance or predict market trends. Or perhaps you are an inventory manager wanting to monitor competitors' out-of-stock times. A two-toned, Python-Excel partnership is your go-to ensemble, your in-house 'sherlock'.

Our first step is to deploy Python to rummage through web data. We resort to libraries such as `beautifulsoup4` for static websites or `selenium` for dynamic ones, and `requests` to communicate with the web. Here's a Python script using `beautifulsoup4` to scrape data from a static website:

```python
import requests
from bs4 import BeautifulSoup as bs

# Making a GET request
response = requests.get('https://www.example.com')

# Parsing HTML content
soup = bs(response.content, 'html.parser')

# Finding specific element
stock_prices = soup.find_all('span', class_='stock-price')
```

With Python, we have the ability to dive into the deepest corners of the internet and reemerge with precious nuggets of information. Yet, these nuggets are raw, unnerving and indigestible. They need refining and understanding, so we call upon Excel to take over.

Next, we feed this raw data into Excel's house, using the `pandas` library to export our findings into the Excel world, where Excel's flair for data analysis awaits us:

```python
#import pandas as pd

# Writing the data
data = pd.DataFrame(stock_prices)
data.to_excel('StockPrices.xlsx')
```

The stage is set for Excel, the maestro of data manipulation and analysis, to do what it does best: breathe sense into numbers and weave a story out of the raw, unrefined data. With its capabilities, you can calculate averages or trends, generate graphs or conduct comprehensive analyses.

Once mined and refined, the constant monitoring and managing of data continues, under the watchful eye of this Python-Excel combo. With Python, you can code a script to perform these actions at regular intervals, creating an automated machine that never rests - data scraping, analyzing and providing you with much-needed insights at your convenience.

```python
import schedule
import time
```

```
def job():
    # Put your entire code here
    pass

#run job every day at 9am
schedule.every().day.at("09:00").do(job)

while True:
    schedule.run_pending()
    time.sleep(1)
` ` `
```

And voila, you've just demystified the intrigue of data scraping and analysis with Python and Excel. A perfect harmonious symphony of code, signals, numbers, graphs, and patterns that sets the stage for not just any data journey, but your data journey. Up next, we unfurl the curtains to another practical chapter of our Python-Excel duet with inventory management systems.

Subsection 11.4b: Inventory Management System (480 words):

No longer condemned to the realms of mere notions, an automated Inventory Management System (IMS) navigates the labyrinth of inventory complexities, making it a vital tool in your arsenal. Under the combined might of Python and Excel, inventory management no longer becomes an intimidating challenge; it morphs into a manageable, systematic process. This dynamic duo, with its knack for linking data-crunching capabilities, hampers the spiraling down inventory glitches and uplifts the core of inventory controls.

A potent Python and Excel concoction can extract, streamline, and integrate inventory-related data into an Excel workbook, serving as an IMS. This synergistic system can do wonders, tracking inventory levels, maintaining records, and ensuring an organized business. Imagine the boon of having such an automated tool in your hand, available at your command and under your control!

Python, the multiskilled toolkit, conquers backend challenges. First, it scrapes inventory data, say, from a given website or API or some data source. Librearies such as `beautifulsoup4`, `request`, and `selenium` come into play here. Post the data extraction process, the data may need cleaning and organizing. Python steps up once again; it uses the `pandas` library to cleanse and condition the data in a structured format.

```python
import requests
from bs4 import BeautifulSoup as bs
import pandas as pd

# Scraping data
response = requests.get('https://www.example.com')
soup = bs(response.content, 'html.parser')
item_stock = soup.find_all('span', class_='item-stock')

# Data cleaning
data = pd.DataFrame(item_stock)
clean_data = data.apply(pd.to_numeric, errors='coerce')
```

Just when Python's melody begins to fade, Excel takes the baton forward with its rich set of tools capable of transforming this numerical jigsaw into meaningful inventory information. Here, Python proves instrumental again with the `openpyxl` and `pandas` libraries, bridging the transition of data from Python to Excel.

```python
# Importing pandas and openpyxl
import pandas as pd
from openpyxl import Workbook

# Create some data
data = ['ProductID', 'ProductDesc', 'Quantity']
df = pd.DataFrame([data], columns=data)

# Create a Pandas Excel writer using openpyxl as the engine.
writer = pd.ExcelWriter("inventory.xlsx", engine='openpyxl')

# Convert the dataframe to an XlsxWriter Excel object.
df.to_excel(writer, sheet_name='Sheet1')

# Close the Pandas Excel writer and output the Excel file.
writer.save()
```

In Excel, pivoting, filtering, charting, or representing the inventory data can unveil piercing insights. Whether identifying overstocked items, managing stock-outs, planning procurement based on demand forecasts, or detecting anomalies in inventory levels, Excel graciously handles it all.

Lastly, we shouldn't overlook automation. A reliable IMS should automatically report, update, and replenish stock. Python's ability to automate mundane tasks with the help of libraries like `schedule` and `time` bestows continuous monitoring, responding to real-time changes, debunking the dangers of human lag.

```python
import schedule
import time

def job():
    #Main activity of inventory management
    pass

# Schedule the job every day at 08:00.
schedule.every().day.at("08:00").do(job)

while 1:
    schedule.run_pending()
    time.sleep(1)
```

Behold, the stellar fusion of Python and Excel has manifested an efficient Inventory Management System, ready to arm you with precise insights, enabling proactive decision-making in your inventory management endeavors. A step into intelligent inventory management, and a leap towards optimized operations sprinkled with the magic of Python and Excel.

However, our journey doesn't end here. Onward, as we delve into the world of customer data management.

Customer Data Management

As we catapult into the era of exponential data growth, strategic customer data management (CDM) becomes the backbone of successful business operations. A robust CDM system, embellished with the might of Python and Excel, acts as a solid foundation for understanding customer behavior, personalizing services, reinforcing customer engagement, and strengthening business-customer relationships. Meshing the versatile prowess of Python with the user-friendly nature of Excel, we pave the way towards highly efficient, automated customer data management that's both comprehensive and understandable.

The journey commences with Python, an excellent data wrangler, impeccably juggling data scraping, processing, and cleaning. Surfing through customer databases, social media platforms, or APIs, Python scripts fetch pertinent customer data with libraries such as `beautifulsoup4`, `selenium`, `requests`, or `Scrapy`.

```python
import requests
from bs4 import BeautifulSoup as bs
import pandas as pd

# Scrape customer data
response = requests.get('https://www.customerdatabase.example.com')
soup = bs(response.content, 'html.parser')
```

```python
customer_info = soup.find_all('div', class_='customer-info')

# Data Cleaning
data = pd.DataFrame(customer_info)
clean_data = data.apply(pd.to_numeric, errors='ignore')
```

Carrying data sanitation baton next, Python uses `pandas` to remove redundancies, clear null values, standardize data, and usher it into a well-structured, flawless format.

With the raw data refurbished, Python then stages data transfer to Excel using `openpyxl` or `pandas`, abridging the gap between complex data structures and intuitive data visualization.

```python
import pandas as pd
from openpyxl import Workbook

# Transfer data to Excel
df = pd.DataFrame(clean_data)

# Write DataFrame to Excel
writer = pd.ExcelWriter("customer_data.xlsx", engine='openpyxl')
df.to_excel(writer, sheet_name='Customer_Info')

# Save the excel
writer.save()
```

```
` ` `
```

Excel, draped with numerous functionalities, competently renders the clean data from Python. Excel tables, pivot tables, filters, slicers, and charts illuminate hidden patterns, customer trends, purchase behaviours, and valuable insights latent in the data. With easy data segmentation and grouping, special offers and focused marketing initiatives targeted at specific customer cohorts become more achievable.

Automating reports and alerts also streamlines the process of staying up-to-date with customer feedback, changes in purchasing patterns, or fluctuations in customer loyalty, providing a head-start in realizing and tackling potential issues.

```python
import schedule
import time

def job():
    #Main activity of CDM
    pass

# Schedule the job every day at 08:00
schedule.every().day.at("08:00").do(job)

while 1:
    schedule.run_pending()
    time.sleep(1)
```

Sailing upon Python and Excel's conjoint strength begets a powerful CDM tool, an instructive compass that guides towards better customer understanding, tailored services, and business growth. Not just a tool, it's an insightful companion that walks with you as you journey into the stratums of customer behaviour, forging a pathway towards transactional relationships that metamorphose into emotional connections.

The engagement with data throughout the book ranged from resolving terminal complexities to enhancing superior solutions - all unified by Python and Excel's functionalities. Let's recapitulate your learning voyage and plot our course forwards as we step into the subsequent section.

CHAPTER 12:
CONCLUSION AND
GOING BEYOND

What you've Learned

In our expedition thus far, we have traversed through the dynamic landscapes of Python and Excel, unravelling the fineness in their intricate weaves. Our endeavours were underpinned by one primary aspiration – to harness their combined power dynamically and innovatively, unravelling their individual might and interplay.

We began our exploration with the fundamental premises of Python and Excel. Unveiling Python as a first-rate, high-level programming language, we delved into Python's powerful features like its simple syntax, variable types, standard operators, structured programming constructs and its rich set of libraries. Excel, a perennial favourite, was recognized not merely as a static tool for spreadsheets but as a platform abounding in capabilities like advanced mathematical functions, data storage, data manipulation capabilities, impressive charts and graphics, and even basic programming through VBA.

Emphasis was given, not just to Python and Excel as standalone entities, but on their seamless interplay. Understanding Python's ability to read, write and manipulate Excel files was explored in depth, highlighting libraries like openpyxl, pandas and xlrd/xlwt. Throughout our journey, Python repeatedly emerged as an ideal companion for Excel, magnifying Excel's potential by automating tasks, managing datasets, generating real-time data and even showcasing opportunities for heavy statistical analysis.

Our engagement with data- the backbone of Python and Excel - was an exciting episode. Focusing mainly on data management, cleaning, and analysis, we explored the utility of pandas for data wrangling and how Python can be used for complex data manipulations. We moved through descriptive statistics and advanced to quantitative analyses, thereby sharpening our exploratory data analysis competence.

Python's versatility was brought to the fore with the introduction of libraries that integrate it with Excel. Through chapters dedicated to interacting between Python and Excel, we learnt about harnessing Python for managing Excel files, controlling Excel functionalities, automating Excel tasks, and even debugging Python scripts within Excel.

We also reached the intricate corners of data cleaning, a critical practice often underestimated. Understanding how Python can be employed to identify and handle missing values and outliers, as well as transform data was exciting. The significance of using Python for automating tasks like these that can become tedious and monotonous if done manually was made apparent.

Real-world projects added zing to our journey. Exploring practical applications like a financial dashboard, report generation, data scraping and analysis, inventory management system, and customer data management enriched our insight into the dynamism of Python and Excel and their usefulness in practical scenarios.

As we journeyed together, we continually discovered and experimented with the endless possibilities that Python and Excel offer. Whether it is Python's prowess with its various libraries that combine best with Excel's user-friendly interface or the ease that Python brings into Excel's highly organized environment, our expedition has only confirmed that when Python and Excel join forces because sheet indeed happens.

But we aren't done yet. We have much more in store for you in the remaining chapters. As we proceed, we will explore more complex use-cases, delve deeper into Python and Excel's functionality and continuously strive to push the boundaries of what's possible when these two mighty powers join forces.

Resources for further learning

After embarking on such an enriching journey of learning, it is only natural to yearn for even more exploration. While we have taken comprehensive strides to cover the inception and sophisticated aspects of Python and Excel, the world of Python programming and Excel management is vast and ever-evolving. For those of you infused with an insatiable thirst for knowledge, there are limitless resources to further expand your horizons.

Professional literature is an abundant source of deep insights into our subjects. Python's official documentation offers a remarkably authoritative view of Python's capabilities and libraries. Python's versatility is reflected in books like 'Fluent Python' by Luciano Ramalho and 'Python Cookbook' by David

Beazley and Brian K. Jones. In contrast, the world of Excel is vividly described in resources such as 'Excel 2016 Bible' by John Walkenbach or 'Excel Formulas and Functions' by Ken Bluttman.

Online platforms can prove to be invaluable. Renowned websites like Stack Overflow and GitHub are filled with active Python and Excel communities, generating a constant stream of knowledge exchange and troubleshooting tips. Online courses on platforms such as Coursera, Udemy, edX or Khan Academy offer a structured approach to engaging with Python in Excel, with different courses aimed at various difficulty levels.

Regular participation in Python and Excel forums and user groups can provide exposure to a variety of real-world problems and solutions. Mailing lists and Python's Special Interest Groups (SIGs), are valuable places to understand and contribute to Python's development. Excel's tech communities, such as the Microsoft Tech Community or Mr. Excel, engage in detailed discussions and offer help on complex problems.

Intellectual growth often can be fueled by engaging with podcasts and webinar series. Podcast.__init__, Talk Python to Me, and Python Bytes offer deep dives into different Python topics, while Excel-related webinars like those offered by Exceljet offer advanced training.

Open-source projects on platforms like GitHub or GitLab provide a unique perspective into applied Python and Excel. Contributing to projects can augment both your understanding and practical handling of Python and Excel together.

Blogs and vlogs provide bite-sized and often specialized knowledge. Python's prolific online presence results in numerous tutorials, articles, and posts that range from basic

Python handling to advanced programming concepts. Excel's vibrant content ecosystem offers many tutorials and guides that delve into the depths of Excel's features and functions.

In conclusion, the path to mastering Python and Excel intertwines different realms of learning. Yet, whether you wish to dive deeper into coding intricacies, gain more practical exposure, or just stay up-to-date with the latest developments, an array of resources is already at your disposal, awaiting discovery. Remember, the true essence of knowledge lies in continuous learning, in recognizing that the journey of exploration never really ends it only evolves. Our expedition might be reaching its conclusion here, but for you, the avid explorer, this can be just the start of a much grander adventure.

Python and Excel Community

Python and Excel are not standalone tools, they exist within rich and thriving communities. These communities provide their members with support, collaboration opportunities, and shared knowledge which is an integral part of professional development. Let's delve into the world of Python and Excel communities, understanding their vitality and impact on Python-Excel integrations.

Python boasts of having a global community, which includes developers, educators, researchers, and enthusiasts from different domains. The influence of this community is evident in the continual growth of Python and its libraries. Python's official website is a hub for community information with active forums and mailing lists. Python conferences such as the PyCon are organized worldwide, where community members congregate to share their work, learn, and collaborate. There are also local user groups, known as Python User Groups (PUGs), which conduct local meetings and coding sessions to share Python knowledge and experiences.

Excel's community is likewise diverse, comprising of business analysts, finance professionals, educators, data scientists, and more. Excel communities are often found on platforms like Microsoft forums, Mr. Excel forums, and Exceljet. The Excel community is committed to supporting its members through problem-solving, sharing insights, and providing a medium for learning advanced Excel utilities. Conferences like Excel Summit South or London Excel Meetup group events are common places for Excel aficionados to network, share experiences, and learn collectively.

GitHub, as an open-source platform, is particularly pivotal in fostering the growth of the Python-Excel community. Developers regularly upload Python-Excel projects with their source codes, making it a treasure trove for novices and experts. The interaction of the community, through contributing to projects and issue-solving, is a remarkable model of collaborative learning.

Reddit hosts active subreddits for Python (r/python) and Excel (r/excel). The platform fosters interaction, with users sharing their challenges, solutions, and interesting implementations of tools. Additionally, the Python community on StackOverflow, a Q&A platform, has many active users who collectively assist in troubleshooting code errors and providing code optimisations.

Python and Excel communities are notable for their proactiveness in supporting diversity and inclusivity in tech spaces. Several initiatives have been taken to inspire people from diverse backgrounds to learn and master Python and Excel. Specific groups, like PyLadies and Django Girls, aim to increase the participation of women in the Python community.

Both the Python and Excel communities have contributed immensely to an information repository, tackling from niche to universal issues. The communities not only nurture conversations around their respective tool but often discuss the intersection of Python and Excel, enabling users for integrated implementations.

In conclusion, Python and Excel communities aren't just repositories of information; they are dynamic, responsive, and inclusive spaces that continually evolve based on their members' needs and contributions. To further deepen your understanding and mastery of Python and Excel's integrated applications, partaking in these communities can be an enriching and enlightening experience. Go forth, and engage in these thriving communities of like-minded enthusiasts who share your passion for Python and Excel.

Python and Excel in the Job Market

As screen dividings dissolve and data becomes the backbone of businesses, the intersection of Python and Excel becomes an increasingly sought-after skillset in the job market. From data analysts and financial modelers to systems engineers and growth hackers, a growing legion of roles now necessitates a fluency in Python-Excel integrations. Let's explore how these formidable tools open new doors in the job market.

Python, crowned as one of the most popular programming languages, is a staple in many fields due to its simplicity, robust library support, and diverse applications. Meanwhile, Excel, a classic tool in the business world, continues to be a reliable workhorse for data management, financial modeling, reporting, and much more. By utilising Python and Excel in unison, one unlocks a powerful hybrid tool, deepening data analysis capabilities, enhancing automation, and ultimately straddling the worlds of programming and business with ease.

In the realm of data science, powerhouse roles such as Data Analysts, Data Scientists, and Machine Learning Engineers have Python as an essential technical requirement. This is supplemented by a proficiency in Excel, which facilitates data cleaning, preliminary analysis and storytelling through its charting capabilities. By using libraries like Pandas to manipulate data and Matplotlib for visualisations, data practitioners are overcoming Excel's performance threshold and adding a layer of sophistication to their analysis.

Financial analysts are another group that are reaping benefits from Python-Excel fluency. In addition to traditional Excel-based financial modeling, analysts are leveraging Python's capabilities for tasks such as running simulations, creating advanced analytical models, automating redundant tasks, and more. For instance, a Monte Carlo simulation that can be a daunting task in Excel can be implemented more efficiently with Python's NumPy library.

In domains like supply chain and operations, Python-Excel skills are leveraged for optimising logistic models, forecast inventory, and managing production schedules. Marketing managers utilise these skills for campaign analysis, customer segmentation, and predicting consumer trends, while for HR professionals, they assist in talent analytics, compensation modeling and predictive retention analysis.

Additionally, knowing how to automate Excel tasks using Python can make you an invaluable asset to any team. Rather than spending long hours on mundane tasks, you can create Python scripts to automate these operations, freeing up time to focus on higher-level analysis or strategy.

Python and Excel integration skills are equally relevant to a host of other job roles, including but not limited to risk managers who need to assess myriad risk factors, project managers planning resource allocation or software developers testing their products.

Learning Python and Excel doesn't just add to your technical skillset; it signals to potential employers that you can straddle diverse workflows, have deep analytical capabilities, and are proficient in tools key to business decision-making processes.

To conclude, Python and Excel combined offer a lucrative skill set that is demanded across a wide spectrum of roles and industries. By mastering the capabilities of both tools, you're not only future-proofing your career, but also opening doors to roles that can significantly impact the business world. When it comes to the Python and Excel skill set, the job market's cry has never been clearer: The demand is hot, and supply is lagging. The stage is set for Python-Excel maestros to shine.

Final Words: The Power of Python and Excel Combined

In the gleaming domain of computing, development, and analytics, Python and Excel emerge as two luminaries, each with their individual strengths and capabilities. Yet, when these titans are interlinked, they form a potent synergy that propels data management and analysis to uncharted territories. Let's delve into the cogent unfolding of the combined prowess of Python and Excel, a saga that revolutionizes the way we perceive automation and data wisdom.

Python, in its elegant simplicity and potent functionality, emerges as a language of choice for varied applications. From scripting to web development, from machine learning to data mining, Python adopts many guises, fitting snugly into every role it is cast into. Its rich ecosystem of libraries extends its native capabilities, empowering it to meet, and often exceed, the challenging demands of today's data-centric world.

On the other hand, Excel, the veteran spreadsheet wrangler, continues to be the cornerstone in countless business operations. It simplifies data wrangling, makes number crunching intuitive, and brings advanced mathematical modeling within the reach of the everyday user. With its extensive array of built-in functions and capabilities, Excel remains an omnipresent force in offices around the globe.

Used in isolation, both Python and Excel exhibit formidable power. However, when combined, they collude to push the boundaries of what's possible in automation, data analysis, and reporting. They allow us to perform complex operations with ease and generate insights from data like never before.

Automation, which is a key strength of these combined tools, brings significant efficiency in terms of time and resources. Instead of manually sifting through spreadsheets, you can unleash Python scripts to do the job in a fraction of the time, reducing the margin of error and freeing up resources for more strategic tasks. Python, when used in conjunction with Excel, can autonomously manipulate spreadsheets, read and write data, and even perform complex mathematical operations.

Python's strength comes to the fore when dealing with large datasets. While Excel can become sluggish under such strains, Python, with its powerful libraries like Pandas and NumPy, effortlessly handles extensive data operations, delivering results with blazing speed and unerring precision.

The alliance of Python and Excel also empowers you to extend the capabilities of your data visualizations. Leveraging Python's Matplotlib and Seaborn libraries, you can create advanced, interactive, and aesthetically pleasing charts and graphs that are miles ahead of the static creations confined to Excel's ecosystem.

We hope that this book has provided you an enlightening journey through the synergistic world of Python and Excel. As we sail towards an era increasingly anchored in data, the power to harness the strength of Python and Excel will remain a prized asset. Whether you are an analyst sharpening your tools or a seasoned developer exploring new landscapes, the coupled strengths of Python and Excel will remain an invaluable companion in your voyage. So, remain curious, stay inventive, and continue to ride the fascinating wave of Python and Excel. The future is promising, and it beckons you with endless possibilities.

www.ingramcontent.com/pod-product-compliance
Lightning Source LLC
LaVergne TN
LVHW051240050326
832903LV00028B/2485